d it is remarkable ... e

...es on existing unofficially, as it

..., in the very heart of London.

George Orwell

...ght that if
...hoice of my
...t should have
...of earth, well
...d market for
...he garden
...ferson

Chance was to work in the garden
where he would care for plan...
and grasses and trees which grew
there peacefully. He would be
as one of them: quiet, openhearted
in the sunshine and heavy
when it rained.

Jerzy Kosinski

...ace in

...and to

...f the

...h, and,

...corner

They set great store by their
gardens. In them they have vineyards, al...
manner of fruit, herbes and flowers, so plea...
ant, well-furnished and finely kept.

Sir Thomas More

GARDENS

How fair is a garden amid
the toils and passions
of existence.

Benjamin
Disraeli

...

place of s...

peace,

Every leaf,

every flower

GARDENS

QUOTATIONS ON THE
PERENNIAL PLEASURES OF
SOIL, SEED, AND SUN

COMPILED BY HOLLY HUGHES
ILLUSTRATED BY MARY WOODIN

By a garden is

meant mystically a

spiritual repose, stillness,

refreshment, delight.

John Henry

Cardinal Newman

RUNNING PRESS
PHILADELPHIA • LONDON

Canadian representatives: General Publishing Co., Ltd.,
30 Lesmill Road, Don Mills, Ontario M3B 2T6.

9 8 7 6 5 4 3 2 1
Digit on the right indicates the number of this printing.

Library of Congress Cataloging-in-Publication Number 93–87591

ISBN 1–56138–457–7

Cover and interior design by Paul Kepple
Cover and interior illustration by Mary Woodin
Edited by Melissa Stein
Typography: ITC Berkeley with Carpenter and Schneidler Initials by Deborah Lugar
Printed in Malaysia

This book may be ordered by mail from the publisher.
Please add $2.50 for postage and handling. *But try your bookstore first!*

Running Press Book Publishers
125 South Twenty-second Street
Philadelphia, Pennsylvania 19103–4399

CONTENTS

ANYONE WHO HAS EVER fallen under the spell of a garden knows what an obsession it can be. It's a very particular passion, rooted in one plot of earth. You may admire or envy other people's gardens, but your own garden is where your heart is.

Your love affair will be full of ups and downs depending on the weather, the terrain, the local pests, the seeds and bulbs you bought—but it will bring you into the cycle of living things in a very vivid and personal way.

Does your heart race on winter afternoons as you pore over seed catalogs? Do you wake up in the middle of the night with an inspiration about where to move those bulbs? Are your fingernails chipped and your neck sunburned from constant weeding? Do you harbor murderous impulses towards aphids, beetles, slugs, or squirrels? In August, do you unload armloads of tomatoes and zucchini upon co-workers, friends, and family?

Well, you're not alone. Through the ages, princes and presidents, artists and writers, doctors and architects, homemakers and historians, scientists and saints have all loved their gardens—and this book brings to you some of their reflections. Each perspective helps you see the garden in a new light, as a living bit of landscape, whether it's Henry David Thoreau's bean-rows or Vita Sackville-West's magnificent Sissinghurst gardens, Claude Monet's water lily ponds or Frances Hodgson Burnett's miraculous secret garden.

These words reveal the garden in all kinds of weather, all times of day, and all seasons of the year. You'll read of the planning of gardens, their sights and scents, and the aches, blisters, and sweat of tending them—all the joys and frustrations that come of caring for any living thing.

Whether your garden is a windowsill jungle, a vegetable garden that provides food all summer, a Zen-inspired arrangement of rocks and mosses, or an elaborate formal landscape that's an ongoing work of art, you'll delight in the rich, vibrant experience of *Gardens*.

AN ENCHANTED SPOT

How fair is a garden amid the toils and passions of existence.
BENJAMIN DISRAELI

When at last I took the time to look into the heart of a
flower, it opened up a whole new world—a world where every
country walk would be an adventure, where every garden
would become an enchanted one. . . .
PRINCESS GRACE OF MONACO

The fine old place never looked more like a delightful home than at that
moment: the great white lilies were in flower; the nasturtiums, their
pretty leaves all silvered with dew, were running away over the low stone
wall; the very noises all around had a heart of peace within them.
GEORGE ELIOT

Through the open door
A drowsy smell of flowers—gray heliotrope
And white sweet clover, and shy mignonette
Comes faintly in, and silent chorus leads
To the pervading symphony of Peace.
JOHN GREENLEAF WHITTIER

By a garden is meant mystically a place of spiritual repose, stillness, peace, refreshment, delight.

JOHN HENRY CARDINAL NEWMAN

Every leaf, every flower in the garden lay open, motionless, as if exhausted, and a sweet, rich, rank smell filled the quivering air. Out of the thick, fleshy leaves of a cactus there rose an aloe stem loaded with pale flowers that looked as though they had been cut out of butter; light flashed upon the lifted spears of the palms; over a bed of scarlet waxen flowers some big black insects "zoom-zoomed"; a great, gaudy creeper, orange splashed with jet, sprawled against a wall.

KATHERINE MANSFIELD

What is the magic of old gardens? Can it be in part that those who designed them had another object in mind besides that of pleasing the eye, which tends to be our only criterion? Perhaps plants had more personality, more dignity, more mystery, when they were held in respect, even in awe, because of the wonderful powers they were supposed to possess.

BRIDGET BOLAND

How I would love to be transported into a scented Elizabethan garden with herbs and Honeysuckles, a knot garden and Roses clambering over a simple arbour. . . .

ROSEMARY VEREY

Chance was to work in the garden, where he would care for plants and grasses and trees which grew there peacefully. He would be as one of them: quiet, openhearted in the sunshine and heavy when it rained.

JERZY KOSINSKI

For the garden is not only a place in which to make things grow and to display the beautiful flowers of the earth, but a place that should accord with the various moods of its admirers. It should be a place in which to hold light banter, a place in which to laugh, and, besides, should have a hidden corner in which to weep.

ALICE LOUNSBERRY

The mute bird sitting on the stone,
The dank moss dripping from the wall,
The garden-walk with weeds o'ergrown,
I love them—How I love them all!

EMILY BRONTË

They set great store by their gardens. In them they have vineyards, all manner of fruit, herbes and flowers, so pleasant, well-furnished and fynely kept.

SIR THOMAS MORE

I have often thought that if heaven had given me choice of my position and calling, it should have been on a rich spot of earth, well watered, and near a good market for the productions of the garden.

THOMAS JEFFERSON

It is well and sadly known, of course, that tens of thousands of individual house lots have not been planted. In other words these houses have not been converted into homes.

FRANK A. WAUGH

"Dear Basia," I write, "I am sitting at a window looking out on a garden in which there is a cherry tree, an apple tree, and bushes of roses now in bloom. The roses are smaller and wilder here, but imagine! All this in the middle of a city."

EVA HOFFMAN

Indeed it is remarkable how Nature goes on existing unofficially, as it were, in the very heart of London.

GEORGE ORWELL

Emerging from city streets where the seasons have for months dragged so sluggishly as to seem unchangeable, he finds in the country that all the signs of rebirth have burst upon him together—the daffodils nodding in the breeze and the primroses glimmering by the roadside, new buds breaking, birds in full song.

A. S. BYATT

God almighty esteemed the life of a man in the garden the happiest he could give him, or else He would not have placed Adam in that of Eden.

SIR WILLIAM TEMPLE

Who loves a garden still his Eden keeps,
Perennial pleasures plants, and wholesome harvest reaps.

BRONSON ALCOTT

Here at the fountain's sliding foot,
Or at some fruit tree's mossy root,
Casting the body's vest aside,
My soul into the boughs does glide.

ANDREW MARVELL

The sanctity and reserve of these front yards of our grandmothers was somewhat emblematic of woman's life of that day: it was restricted, and narrowed to a small outlook and monotonous likeness to her neighbor's; but it was a life easily satisfied with small pleasures, and it was comely and sheltered and carefully kept, and pleasant to the home household; and these were no mean things.

ALICE MORSE EARLE

Everything in this suburb reminded one of the gardens of childhood. Pink petals drifted along damp pavements, and through my window I caught the harsh smell of the earth, sour after a long cold winter. The trees were still leafless and the weather uncertain, but . . . the white light seemed to promise long evenings and a quick flowering.

ANITA BROOKNER

For love of flowers every blooming square in cottage gardens seen from the flying windows of the train has its true and touching message for the traveller; every bush and tree in nearer field and farther wood becomes an object of delight and stirs delightful thought.

FRANCIS KING

What is all this juice and all this joy?
A strain of the earth's sweet being in the beginning
In Eden garden.

GERARD MANLEY HOPKINS

BEHOLD, THE GARDENER

Show me your garden and I shall tell you what you are.

ALFRED AUSTIN

GARDENS

I am . . . as fond of my garden as a young author of his first play when it has been well receiv'd by the town. . . .

LADY MARY WORTLEY MONTAGU

Each one has his own most real thing. Mine is the garden.

LOUISA YEOMANS KING

You can spot real gardeners as easily in January as in July. Bright seed catalogs cover their coffee tables. A couple of catalogs lie on the kitchen table beside the toast and jam. There are a few on the bedside table in case of insomnia.

RUTH PAGE

There are golf bores, political bores and many other types of bores. I most certainly am a garden bore.

VISCOUNT BLAKENHAM

I am not a greedy person except about flowers and plants, and then I am afraid I become fanatically greedy.

MAY SARTON

For my business I have to travel a lot. But it would have to be something very important to keep me away from my garden at Easter and in June.

HARDY AMIES

All gardeners know better than other gardeners.
CHINESE PROVERB

"I warned you to use plenty of wisteria lavender and sweet-pea pink," said an experienced gardener at the time, surveying my dull effect and quite pleased (for gardeners are not angels, let me tell you) to see it had worked out as badly as she had predicted.
HENRY MITCHELL

They tended their lawns with reverence, buying rotating sprinklers and hoses with holes along their lengths so that the water made little arcs of diamonds in the sunshine.
ANNA QUINDLEN

"My brother and sister will be enchanted with this place. People who have extensive grounds themselves are always pleased with any thing in the same style."

Emma doubted the truth of this sentiment. She had a great idea that people who had extensive grounds themselves cared very little for the extensive grounds of any body else. . . .
JANE AUSTEN

In general, it is to be observed that men plow while women sow; prune fruit and nut trees but leave the harvest to women; and most men like working with vegetables (all, that is, but the weeding).
ELEANOR PERÉNYI

"John says he never cares about the flowers of 'em, but men have no eye for anything neat. He says his favorite flower is a cauliflower."
THOMAS HARDY

Although many males from fourteen to fifty fight in the emperor's army or climb the rigging of the emperor's ships, the remaining males together with children and women plough, dig, plant seed, carry water, weed, and harvest. Thus in the suburbs we rake leaves together; thus we trim the forsythia; thus we arrange a sprinkler on the suburban lawn, edge the grass neatly against the sidewalk, mow, and mulch.
DONALD HALL

I am a lazy gardener, subscribing to the view that no man should have a garden larger than his wife can take care of. However, there has to be a compromise, for my spouse, curiously, feels that no woman should have a garden larger than her husband can tend.
FREDERICK MCGOURTY

Millions of women between the ages of forty-five and fifty-five discover gardening. Other people imagine that this is because they have nothing else to do. In fact there is always something else to do, as every woman who gardens knows.
GERMAINE GREER

All gardeners know better than other gardeners.
CHINESE PROVERB

"I warned you to use plenty of wisteria lavender and sweet-pea pink," said an experienced gardener at the time, surveying my dull effect and quite pleased (for gardeners are not angels, let me tell you) to see it had worked out as badly as she had predicted.
HENRY MITCHELL

They tended their lawns with reverence, buying rotating sprinklers and hoses with holes along their lengths so that the water made little arcs of diamonds in the sunshine.
ANNA QUINDLEN

"My brother and sister will be enchanted with this place. People who have extensive grounds themselves are always pleased with any thing in the same style."

    Emma doubted the truth of this sentiment. She had a great idea that people who had extensive grounds themselves cared very little for the extensive grounds of any body else. . . .
JANE AUSTEN

In general, it is to be observed that men plow while women sow; prune fruit and nut trees but leave the harvest to women; and most men like working with vegetables (all, that is, but the weeding).
ELEANOR PERÉNYI

"John says he never cares about the flowers of 'em, but men have no eye for anything neat. He says his favorite flower is a cauliflower."

THOMAS HARDY

Although many males from fourteen to fifty fight in the emperor's army or climb the rigging of the emperor's ships, the remaining males together with children and women plough, dig, plant seed, carry water, weed, and harvest. Thus in the suburbs we rake leaves together; thus we trim the forsythia; thus we arrange a sprinkler on the suburban lawn, edge the grass neatly against the sidewalk, mow, and mulch.

DONALD HALL

I am a lazy gardener, subscribing to the view that no man should have a garden larger than his wife can take care of. However, there has to be a compromise, for my spouse, curiously, feels that no woman should have a garden larger than her husband can tend.

FREDERICK MCGOURTY

Millions of women between the ages of forty-five and fifty-five discover gardening. Other people imagine that this is because they have nothing else to do. In fact there is always something else to do, as every woman who gardens knows.

GERMAINE GREER

When Mrs. Harling made garden that spring, we could feel the stir of her undertaking through the willow hedge that separated our place from hers.
WILLA CATHER

There was a towering elm in the front lawn and another as tall in the back overlooking an English garden, a romantic geometry of curved beds around a birdbath before a pair of flowering quince. Here my mother would come into her own, nurturing, with the same driving energy she applied to her piano and kitchen, a garden like an Anglo-Chinese dream.
ELEANOR MUNRO

She, who was in every other way so reserved, so delicately poised, became a different person out of doors, as if she shed a skin when she knelt by a border in one of those big straw hats tied under her chin with a chiffon scarf, and weeded fiercely.
MAY SARTON

. . . We encountered Aunt Dahlia, who, wearing that hat of hers that looks like one of those baskets you carry fish in, was messing about in the herbaceous border by the tennis lawn.
P. G. WODEHOUSE

[After her house burned down,] Miss Maudie's sunhat was suspended in a thin layer of ice, like a fly in amber, and we had to dig under the dirt for her hedge-clippers. We found her in her back yard, gazing at her frozen charred azaleas.

"We're bringing back your things, Miss Maudie," said Jem. "We're awful sorry."

Miss Maudie looked around, and the shadow of her old grin crossed her face. "Always wanted a smaller house, Jem Finch. Gives me more yard. Just think, I'll have more room for my azaleas now!"

HARPER LEE

I like to think of old gardeners pottering their life-time away in green baize aprons, straw hats, a twist of raffia behind their ears, and a Nannie-like intimacy with the plants under their care.

VITA SACKVILLE-WEST

. . . And the loving pride with which this grand old gardener pointed out to us the particular merits of this or that pet can be appreciated only by those whose lives have been lived in close companionship with plants.

ERNEST H. WILSON

I am once more seated under my own vine and fig-tree . . . and hope to spend the remainder of my days . . . in peaceful retirement; making political pursuits yield to the more rational amusement of cultivating the earth.

GEORGE WASHINGTON

I think it is because I have been more or less a gardener all my life that
I still feel like a child in many ways, although from the number of years
I have lived I ought to know that I am quite an old woman.

GERTRUDE JEKYLL

Who is the happy gardener? It is he that hath the hope and the
resignation of a gambler, the nerves of a circus acrobat, the
unfading wonderment of a growing child, the detachment of a
seer, and, above all, the forbearance of the eldest of the Pan-
davas.

R. K. NARAYAN

Yes, of course he'd seen the old man before, always outside, walking
with his quick stoop, raking leaves, watering trees, pestering the
gardener. He'd live another thirty years.

WALKER PERCY

Among gardeners, enthusiasm and experience rarely exist in
equal measures. The beginner dreams of home-grown bouquets
and baskets of ripe fruit, the veteran of many seasons has
learned to expect slugs, mildew, and frost.

ROGER SWAIN

The garden shudders when it hears the back door slam and recognizes
my footsteps upon the back porch. By now it knows the man it is dealing
with: a harsh but just master who brooks no nonsense from flora or weed.

RUSSELL BAKER

A neighbor suggests, that I might put up a scarecrow near the vines, which would keep the birds away. I am doubtful about it: the birds are too much accustomed to seeing a person in poor clothes in the garden to care much for that.

CHARLES DUDLEY WARNER

... Adam was a gardener, and God who made him sees
That half a proper gardener's work is done upon his knees.

RUDYARD KIPLING

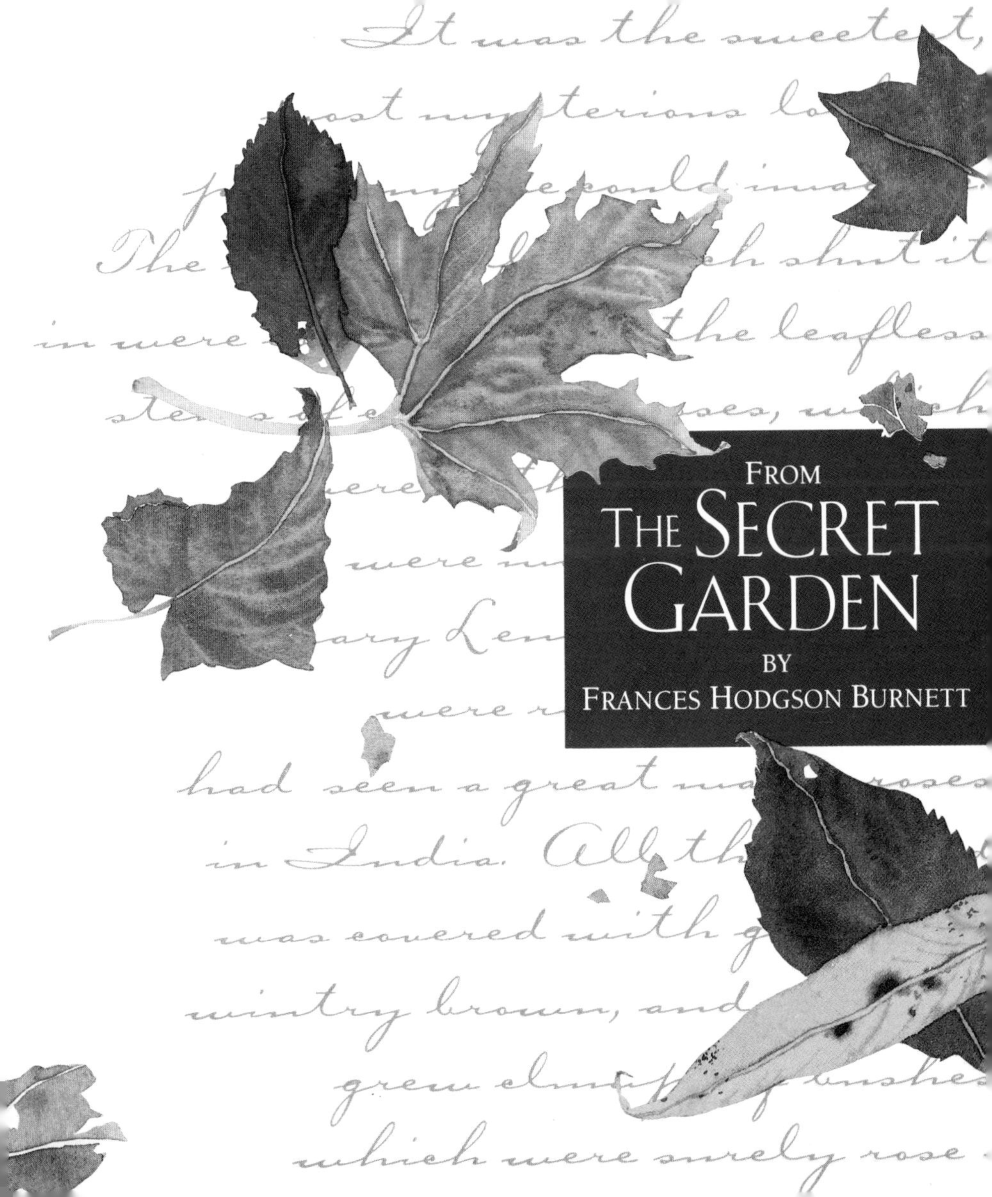

FROM

THE SECRET GARDEN

BY

FRANCES HODGSON BURNETT

IT WAS THE SWEETEST, most mysterious-looking place anyone could imagine. The high walls which shut it in were covered with the leafless stems of climbing roses, which were so thick that they were matted together. Mary Lennox knew they were roses because she had seen a great many roses in India. All the ground was covered with grass of a wintry brown, and out of it grew clumps of bushes which were surely rose-bushes if they were alive. There were numbers of standard roses which had so spread their branches that they were like little trees. There were other trees in the garden, and one of the things which made the place look strangest and loveliest was that climbing roses had run all over them and swung down long tendrils which made light swaying curtains, and here and there they had caught at each other or at a far-reaching branch and had crept from one tree to another and made lovely bridges of themselves. There were neither leaves nor roses on them now, and Mary did not know whether they were dead or alive, but their thin grey or brown branches looked like a sort of hazy mantle spreading over everything, walls, and trees, and even brown grass, where they had fallen from their fastenings and run along the ground. It was this hazy tangle from tree to tree which made it look so mysterious. Mary had thought it must be different from other gardens which had not been left by themselves so long; and, indeed, it was different from any other place she had ever seen in her life.

"How still it is!" she whispered. "How still!"

Then she waited a moment and listened at the stillness. The robin, who had flown to his tree-top, was still as all the rest. He did not even flutter his wings; he sat without stirring, and looked at Mary.

"No wonder it is still," she whispered again. "I am the first person who has spoken in here for ten years."

She moved away from the door, stepping as softly as if she were afraid of awakening someone. She was glad that there was grass under her feet and that her steps made no sounds. She walked under one of the fairy-like arches between the trees and looked up at the sprays and tendrils which formed them.

"I wonder if they are all quite dead," she said. "Is it all a quite dead garden? I wish it wasn't."

If she had been Ben Weatherstaff she could have told whether the wood was alive by looking at it, but she could only see that there were only grey or brown sprays and branches, and none showed any signs of even a tiny leaf-bud anywhere.

But she was *inside* the wonderful garden, and she could come through the door under the ivy any time, and she felt as if she had found a world all her own.

The sun was shining inside the four walls and the high arch of blue sky over this particular piece of Misselthwaite seemed even more brilliant and soft than it was over the moor. The robin flew down from his tree-top and hopped about or flew after her from one bush to another. He chirped a good deal and had a very busy air, as if he were showing her things. Everything was strange and silent, and she seemed to be hundreds of miles away from anyone, but somehow she did not feel lonely at all. All that troubled her was her wish that she knew whether all the roses were dead, or if perhaps some of them had lived and might put out leaves and buds as the weather got warmer. She did not want it to be a quite dead garden. If it were a quite alive garden, how wonderful it would be, and what thousands of roses would grow on every side?

Her skipping-rope had hung over her arm when she came in, and after she had walked about for awhile she thought she would skip round the whole garden, stopping when she wanted to look at things. There seemed to have been grass paths here and there, and in one or two corners there were alcoves of evergreen with stone seats or all moss-covered flower-urns in them.

As she came near the second of these alcoves she stopped skipping. There had once been a flower bed in it, and she thought she saw something sticking out of the black earth—some sharp little pale green points. She remembered what Ben Weatherstaff had said, and she knelt down to look at them.

"Yes, they are tiny growing things and they might be crocuses or snowdrops of daffodils," she whispered.

She bent very close to them and sniffed the fresh scent of the damp earth. she liked it very much.

"Perhaps there are some other ones coming up in some other places," she said. "I will go all over the garden and look."

She did not skip, but walked. She went slowly and kept her eyes on the ground. She looked in the old border-beds and among the grass, and after she had gone round, trying to miss nothing, she had found ever so many more sharp, pale green points, and she had become quite excited again.

"It isn't a quite dead garden," she cried out softly to herself. "Even if the roses are dead, there are other things alive."

She did not know anything about gardening, but the grass seemed so thick in some of the places where the green points were pushing their way through that she thought they did not seem to have room enough to grow. She searched around until she found a rather sharp piece of wood and knelt down and dug and weeded out the weeds and grass until she had made nice little clear places around them.

"Now they look as if they can breathe," she said, after she had finished with the first ones. "I am going to do ever so many more. I'll do all I can see. If I haven't time today I can come tomorrow."

She went from place to place, and dug and weeded, and enjoyed herself so immensely that she was led on from bed to bed and into the grass under the trees. The exercise made her so warm that she first threw her coat off, and then her hat, and without knowing it she was smiling down on to the grass and the pale green points all the time.

The robin was tremendously busy. He was very much pleased to see gardening begun on his own estate. He had often wondered at Ben Weatherstaff. Where gardening is done all sorts of delightful things to eat are turned up with the soil. Now here was this new kind of creature who was not half Ben's size and yet had the sense to come into his garden and begin at once.

Mistress Mary worked in her garden until it was time to go to her midday dinner. In fact she was rather late in remembering, when she put on her coat and hat and picked up her skipping-rope, she could not believe that she had been working two or three hours. She had been actually happy all the time; and dozens and dozens of the tiny, pale green points were to be seen in cleared places, looking twice as cheerful as they had looked before when the grass and weeds had been smothering them.

"I shall come back this afternoon," she said, looking round at her new kingdom, and speaking to the trees and rose-bushes as if they heard her.

Then she ran lightly across the grass, pushed open the slow old door, and slipped through it under the ivy.

WORKING THE SOIL

To a certain extent we raise a garden as we might a child, putting in the seed, nourishing it and gathering nourishment from it, pruning and weeding its growth, protecting it, loving it, worrying over it.

ROBERT FINCH

Removing the weeds, putting fresh soil about the bean stems, and encouraging this weed which I had sown, making the yellow soil express its summer thought in bean leaves and blossoms rather than in wormwood and piper and millet grass, making the earth say beans instead of grass,—this was my daily work.

HENRY DAVID THOREAU

. . . They who labor in the earth are the chosen people of God.

THOMAS JEFFERSON

I passed by the field of a sluggard,
by the vineyard of a man without sense;
and lo, it was all overgrown with thorns;
the ground was covered with nettles,
and its stone wall broken down.

PROVERBS, 24: 30-31

There is nothing pleasanter than spading when the ground is soft and damp.
JOHN STEINBECK

All through the long winter I dream of my garden. On the first warm day of spring I dig my fingers deep into the soft earth. I can feel its energy, and my spirits soar.
HELEN HAYES

She hitched up her skirt and attacked the nearest row of lavender, gathering the long stems into a tight bunch with one arm and slicing them off at the bottom with a single smooth pull of the sickle. In five minutes she had cut more than I had in an hour. It looked easy; bend, gather, pull. Nothing to it.
PETER MAYLE

I don't dislike gardeners but I'd be just as pleased with them if they didn't go around trying to make me feel as if I hated nature. I don't hate it. I just don't like to grovel in the dirt.
ANDY ROONEY

It would have astonished Madame de Normandin to know that a woman like my aunt spent hours of every day digging and weeding, and dead-heading and transplanting, and trundling wheelbarrows down muddy paths. She frequently spoke of the wonders of British gardens. . . . But *why* English gardens were so green and colorful and abundant was probably a mystery.
A. N. WILSON

The flowers were like new acquaintances; she approached them in a familiar spirit, and made herself at home among them. The garden walks were damp, and Edna called to the maid to bring out her rubber sandals. And there she stayed, and stayed, digging around the plants, trimming, picking dead dry leaves.

KATE CHOPIN

Some people are like ants. Give them a warm day and a piece of ground and they start digging. There the similarity ends. Ants keep on digging. Most people don't. They establish contact with the soil, absorb so much vernal vigor that they can't stay in one place, and desert the fork or spade to see how the rhubarb is coming and whether the asparagus is yet in sight.

HAL BORLAND

There is a lovable quality about the actual tools. One feels so kindly to the thing that enables the hand to obey the brain. Moreover, one feels a good deal of respect for it; without it brain and hand would be helpless.

GERTRUDE JEKYLL

Men can't be trusted with pruning shears any more than they can be trusted with the grocery money in a delicatessen. . . . They are like boys with new pocket knives who will not stop whittling.

PHYLLIS MCGINLEY

Your first job is to prepare the soil. The best tool for this is your neighbor's motorized garden tiller. If your neighbor does not own a garden tiller, suggest that he buy one.

DAVE BARRY

In March and in April from morning till night
In sowing and seeding good housewives delight.

THOMAS TUSSER

I do not know what you have been doing this morning; for my part, I have been in the dew up to my knees, laying lindens.

MADAME DE SEVIGNÉ

You're supposed to get tired planting bulbs. But it's an agreeable tiredness.

GAIL GODWIN

I guess a good gardener always starts as a good weeder.

AMOS PETTINGILL

It takes me longer to weed than most people, because I will do it so thoroughly. It is such a pleasure and satisfaction to clear the beautiful brown earth, smooth and soft, from these rough growths, leaving the beautiful green Poppies and Larkspurs and Pinks and Asters, and the rest, in undisturbed possession!

CELIA THAXTER

Soon her fingers were deftly pulling out tufts of grass and violets from around the bleeding heart; nothing like weeding to unknot the mind. . . .

MAY SARTON

To move down a line of flowers, inch by inch, pulling weeds, and to be able an hour or two later—who could tell how much time had passed?—to look back and see the flowers standing by themselves against the brown soil, gave me a feeling of joy different from any I had known.

JAY NEUGEBOREN

You can get out in the garden and bend over to weed, and literal brow sweat will drop off onto the loam. The vegetables like it.

ROY BLOUNT, JR.

And speaking of kneeling, allow me to mention that most afflicted portion of the gardener's anatomy, the knee. Obviously when the knee was designed, no thought was given to kneeling; or if it was, the assumption was to make it as uncomfortable as possible.

PETER LOEWER

. . . What we by day
Lop overgrown, or prune, or prop, or bind,
One night or two with wanton growth derides
Tending to wild.

JOHN MILTON

We have a little garden,
A garden of our own,
And every day we water there
The seeds that we have sown.

We love our little garden,
And tend it with such care,
You will not find a faded leaf
Or blighted blossom there.

ANONYMOUS NURSERY RHYME,
AS QUOTED IN BEATRIX POTTER'S
CECILY PARSLEY'S NURSERY RHYMES

And her flowers reward her work by their magnificence: peonies whiter than the idea of white and as big as basketballs; hollyhocks seven feet tall with a blossom delicately peach-pink. People swerve and slow down driving by, if they are flower people; we fear accidents.

DONALD HALL

There can be no other occupation like gardening in which, if you were to creep up behind someone at their work, you would find them smiling.

MIRABEL OSLER

Gardening is what we gardeners like to do: digging, fussing with our plants, weeding, deadheading—all the soothing creative labor that goes into maintaining our personal Edens.

PAGE DICKEY

Being happy is dirt under your fingernails, wearing old clothes, having a good idea get better the longer you work at it, starting a new bed, giving plants away, and listening to rain.

GEOFFREY B. CHARLESWORTH

THE SENSES ALIVE

There is not a single colour hidden away in the chalice of a flower. . . to which, by some subtle sympathy with the very soul of things, my nature does not answer.

OSCAR WILDE

I have a friend, an amateur botanist, who carries a sketch pad with her and draws each flower she identifies. There is no surer way, she tells me, of learning a plant, simply because of the painstaking observation needed to put it on paper. She is right, and some day when I have fewer bees and more time I would like to do this too.

SUE HUBBELL

In a way, nobody sees a flower really, it is so small, we haven't time—
and to see takes time, like to have a friend takes time.

GEORGIA O'KEEFFE

Here rosemary and lavender and ramping geraniums
survived, and a clump of radiant lyrical light-giving
pink-white oleanders which made Tim positively
shudder with colour-experience.

IRIS MURDOCH

I myself am quite absorbed by the . . . delicate yellow, delicate soft green,
delicate violet of a ploughed and weeded piece of soil, regularly chequered
by the green of flowering potato-plants, everything under a sky with
delicate blue, white, pink, violet tones.

VINCENT VAN GOGH

Athwart the wood rises a fount of cottage-smoke from among
mellow and dim roofs. Under the smoke and partly scarfed at
times by a drift from it is the yellow of sunflower and dahlia,
the white of anemone, the tenderest green and palest purple of
a thick cluster of autumn crocuses that have broken out of the
dark earth and stand surprised. . . .

EDWARD THOMAS

I cannot see what flowers are at my feet,
   Nor what soft incense hangs upon the boughs,
But, in embalmed darkness, guess each sweet
   Wherewith the seasonable month endows
The grass, the thicket, and the fruit-tree wild
   White hawthorn, and the pastoral eglantine:
      Fast fading violets covered up in leaves;
        And mid-May's eldest child,
The coming musk-rose, full of dewy wine,
   The murmurous haunt of flies on summer eves.

JOHN KEATS

The flowers never waste their sweetness on the desert air or, for that matter, on the jungle air. In fact, they waste it only when nobody except a human being is there to smell it. It is for the bugs and for a few birds, not for men, that they dye their petals or waft their scents.

JOSEPH WOOD KRUTCH

. . . But every sound is sweet;
Myriads of rivulets hurrying thro' the lawn,
The moan of doves in immemorial elms,
And murmuring of innumerable bees.

ALFRED TENNYSON

. . . In the garden, after a rainfall, you can faintly, yes, hear the breaking of new blooms.

TRUMAN CAPOTE

Here comes the time when, vibrating on its stem, every flower fumes like a censer; noises and perfumes circle in the evening air.

CHARLES BAUDELAIRE

. . . I felt suddenly, as I rose again, a bitter-sweet fragrance of almonds steal towards me from the hawthorn-blossom, and I then noticed that on the flowers themselves were little spots of a creamier colour, in which I imagined that this fragrance must lie concealed, as the taste of an almond cake lay in the burned parts. . . .

MARCEL PROUST

My own nose is not a very good organ, because I am a heavy smoker, but nevertheless I value fragrance and find it one of the charms of a garden, whether indoors or out.

KATHARINE S. WHITE

It is a golden maxim to cultivate the garden for the nose, and the eyes will take care of themselves.

ROBERT LOUIS STEVENSON

When I was a boy, I thought scent was contained in dewdrops on flowers and if I got up very early in the morning, I could collect it and make perfume.

OSCAR DE LA RENTA

Nor is the fragrant garden ever wholly our own. . . . Over hedge or wall, and often far down the highway, it sends a greeting, not alone to us who have toiled for it, but to the passing stranger, the blind beggar, the child skipping to school, the tired woman on her way to work, the rich man, the careless youth.

LOUISE BEEBE WILDER

Can words describe the fragrance of the very breath of spring—that delicious commingling of the perfume of arbutus, the odor of pines, and the snow-soaked soil just warming into life?

NELTJE BLANCHAN

The scent from the garden rises like heat from a body, there must be night-blooming flowers, it's so strong. I can almost see it, red radiation, wavering upwards like the shimmer above highway tarmac at noon.

MARGARET ATWOOD

I sprinted barefoot across the lawn with my favorite playmate, the cook's son, to the stream at the end of the garden. We quarreled in our usual way, waded in the tepid water under the lime trees, and waited for the night to bring out the smell of the jasmine.

SANTHA RAMA RAU

She loved the night-blooming flowers, nicotania and verbena, which filled the summer air with perfume. . . .

ELEANOR MUNRO

The lime trees were in bloom. But in the early morning only a faint fragrance drifted through the garden, an airy message, an aromatic echo of the dreams during the short summer night.

ISAK DINESEN

My very heart faints and my whole soul grieves
At the moist rich smell of the rotting leaves,
        And the breath
        Of the fading edges of box beneath,
And the year's last rose.

ALFRED TENNYSON

But the garden. . . was exhaling scents that were cloying, fleshy, and slightly putrid, like the aromatic liquids distilled from the relics of certain saints; the carnations superimposed their pungence on the formal fragrance of roses and the oily emanations of magnolias drooping in corners; and somewhere beneath it all was a faint smell of mint mingling with a nursery whiff of acacia and the jammy one of myrtle; from a grove beyond the wall came an erotic waft of early orange blossom.

It was a garden for the blind: a constant offense to the eyes, a pleasure strong if somewhat crude to the nose.

GIUSEPPE DI LAMPEDUSA

As for the garden of mint, the very smell of it alone recovers and refreshes our spirits, as the taste stirs up our appetite for meat.

PLINY THE ELDER

Awake, O north wind; and come, O south wind!
Blow upon my garden, let its fragrance be wafted abroad.
Let my beloved come to his garden,
And eat its choicest fruits.

THE SONG OF SOLOMON, 4:16

The tulips I had planted last autumn were in bloom, and I liked to sit and caress their petals, which felt disgustingly delicious, like scraps of peau de soie.

JAMAICA KINCAID

How can one help shivering with delight when one's hot fingers close around the stem of a live flower, cool from the shade and stiff with newborn vigor.

COLETTE

The afternoon sun penetrated the mass of honeysuckle that covered the porch, and fell on my upturned face. My fingers lingered almost unconsciously on the familiar leaves and blossoms which had just come forth to greet the sweet southern spring.

HELEN KELLER

The greatest gift of a
garden is the restoration
of the five senses. During the
first year in the country I
noticed but few birds, t[he]
year I saw a f
by the fourth ye
tree tops, the t
seemed teemin
life. "Where
suddenly
I asked mysel
birds had alw
I had
to see
lind

FROM
LET'S MAKE A
FLOWER
GARDEN
BY
HANNA RION

THE GREATEST GIFT OF A GARDEN

is the restoration of the five senses.

During the first year in the country I noticed but few birds, the second year I saw a few more, but by the fourth year the air, the tree tops, the thickets and ground seemed teeming with bird life. "Where did they all suddenly come from?" I asked myself. The birds had always been there, but I hadn't the power to see; I had been made purblind by the city and only gradually regained my power of sight.

My ears, deafened by the ceaseless whir and din of commerce, had lost the keenness which catches the nuances of bird melody, and it was long before I was aware of distinguishing the varying tones that afterward meant joy, sorrow, loss or love, to me. That hearing has now become so keen, there is no bond of sleep so strong that the note of a strange bird will not pierce to the unsleeping, subconscious ear and arouse me instantly to alertness in every fibre of my being. I wonder if even death will make me insensate to the first chirp of a vanguard robin in March.

During that half-awake first year of country life I was walking with a nature-wise man and as we passed by a field where the cut hay lay wilting, he whiffed and said, "There's a good deal of ragweed in that hay." I gazed on him with the admiration I've saved all my life for wizards and wondered what peculiar brand of nose he had.

Then the heart, the poor jaded heart, that must etherize itself to endure the grimness of city life at all, how subtly it begins throbbing again in unison with the great symphony of the natural. The awakened heart can sense spring in the air when there is no visible suggestion in calendar or frosted earth, and knowing the songful secret, the heart can cause the feet to dance through a day that would only mean winter to an urbanite.

The sense of taste can only be restored by a constant diet of unwilted vegetables and freshly picked fruit.

The delicacy of touch comes back gradually by tending injured birdlings, by the handling of fragile infant plants, and by the acquaintance with different leaf textures, which finally makes one able to distinguish a plant, even in the dark, by its Irish tweed, silken or fur finish.

And the foot, how intangibly it becomes sensitized; how instinctively it avoids a plant even when the eye is busy elsewhere. On the darkest night I can traverse the rocky ravine, the thickets, the sinuous paths through overgrown patches, and never stumble, scratch myself or crush a leaf. My foot knows every unevenness of each individual bit of garden, and adjusts itself lovingly without the conscious thought of brain.

To the ears that have learned to catch the first tentative lute of a marsh frog in spring, orchestras are no longer necessary. To the eyes that have regained their sight, no wonder lies in the craftsmanship of a tiny leaf form of an inconsequential weed, than is to be found in a bombastic arras. To the resuscitated nose is revealed the illimitable secrets of earth incense, the whole gamut of flower perfume, and other fragrant odors too intangible to be classed, odors which wing the spirit to realms our bodies are as yet too clumsy to inhabit.

To the awakened mind there is nothing so lowly in the things below and above ground but can command respect and study. Darwin spent only thirty years on the study of the humble earthworm.

To get the greatest good from a garden we should not undertake more than we can personally take care of. I have not had a gardener since the first year when outside help was necessary for the translation of the sumac and briarpatches of our Wilderness into arable land. A gardener is only helpful for the preliminary work of spading, after that his very presence is profanation.

Garden making is creative work, just as much as painting or writing a poem. It is a personal expression of self, an individual conception of beauty. I should as soon think of asking a secretary to write my book, or the cook to assist in a water color painting, as to permit a gardener to plant or dig among my flowers.

A DAY IN THE GARDEN

I know a little garden close,
Set thick with lily and red rose,
Where I would wander if I might
From dewy morn to dewy night.

WILLIAM MORRIS

The world has different owners at sunrise. . . . Even your own
garden does not belong to you. Rabbits and blackbirds have
the lawns; a tortoise-shell cat who never appears in daytime
patrols the brick walls, and a golden-tailed pheasant glints his
way through the iris spears.

ANNE MORROW LINDBERGH

And it may have been that his only happy moments were these at dawn,
when he went with his dog over the known ways . . . watching as color
gradually emerged from the indistinct gray among the field rows and the
olive branches, and recognizing the song of the morning birds one by one.

ITALO CALVINO

The morning dawns with an unwonted crimson; the flowers
more odorous seem; the garden birds sing louder, and the
laughing sun ascends the gaudy earth with an unusual
brightness: all nature smiles, and the whole world is pleased.

DAY KELLOGG LEE

I pushed the gate that swings so silently,
And I was in the garden and aware
Of early daylight on the flowers there
And cups of dew sun-kindled.

PAUL VERLAINE

Awake, the morning shines, and the fresh field
Calls us; we lose the prime, to mark how spring
Our tended Plants, how blows the Citron Grove,
What drops the Myrrh, and what the balmy Reed,
How Nature paints her colors, how the Bee
Sits on the Bloom extracting liquid sweet.

JOHN MILTON

And at noon he would come
Up from the garden, his hard crooked hands
Gentle with earth, his knees earth-stained, smelling
Of sun, of summer. . . .

ARCHIBALD MACLEISH

The afternoon sun poured down on us through the drying
grape leaves. The orchard seemed full of sun, like a cup, and
we could smell the ripe apples on the trees.

WILLA CATHER

When the sun declined toward the west in the afternoon, I sat in the shade and from the veranda turned the hose with its fine sprinkler all over the garden. Oh, the joy of it! The delicious scents from earth and leaves, the glitter of drops on the young green, the gratitude of all the plants at the refreshing bath and draught of water!

CELIA THAXTER

But the real forays into the unknown were made in other circumstances, like our side porch on summer evenings, when the peonies glowed from the garden beyond, and the elm cast a shadow intricate as a web over the lawn, the hedges, the flower beds.

ELEANOR MUNRO

In the evening calm, hardly a breath of air touched the garden. The heat was intense, and the quiet gave the light and dark greens of the foliage a special limpidity. The green of the lawn seemed to rise up and flow through her.

JUNICHIRO TANIZAKI

But from flowers to stars, is the distance so great? If one stands beside them in the garden in the clear obscure of twilight, and watches the heavenly lights appearing faintly in the darkening sky, an inner feeling recognizes that they belong to the same world of influences, and that we are one with them both.

CANDACE WHEELER

She stared out of the window, which was uncurtained because
Crowe loved to see his cypresses, yews and junipers fade slowly into the
thickening night, because he liked to smell gillyflowers and night-scented
stocks and to watch the white moon sail over his box hedges, over
the white Apollo and Diana poised over the walk which led to
the sunken garden.

A. S. BYATT

She went and stood at an open window and looked out
upon the deep tangle of the garden below. All the mystery
and witchery of the night seemed to have gathered there
amid the perfumes and the dusky and tortuous outlines of
flowers and foliage.

KATE CHOPIN

And, O my garden gleaming cold and white,
Thou hast outshone the far faint moon on high.

YÜAN MEE

How could such sweet and wholesome hours
Be reckoned but with herbs and flowers?

ANDREW MARVELL

HOW DOES YOUR GARDEN GROW?

Of all the wonderful things in the wonderful universe of God, nothing seems to me more surprising that the planting of a seed in the blank earth and the result thereof. Take a Poppy seed, for instance: it lies in your palm, the merest atom of matter, hardly visible, a speck, a pin's point in bulk, but within it is imprisoned a spirit of beauty ineffable, which will break its bonds and emerge from the dark ground and blossom in a splendor so dazzling as to baffle all powers of description.

CELIA THAXTER

"That's the good rich earth," he answered, digging away. "It's in a good humour makin' ready to grow things. It's glad when plantin' time comes. It's dull in the winter when it's got nowt to do. In th' flower gardens out there things will be stirrin' down below in th' dark. Th' sun's warmin' 'em. You'll see bits o' green spikes stickin' out' o' th' black earth after a bit."

FRANCES HODGSON BURNETT

Seldom do we realize that the world is practically no thicker to us than the print of our footsteps on the path. Upon that surface we walk and act our comedy of life, and what is beneath is nothing to us. But it is out

from that under-world, from the dead and the unknown, from the cold moist ground, that these green blades have sprung.

RICHARD JEFFERIES

She was struck by the fertility of the soil; she had seldom been in a garden where the flowers looked so well, and even the weeds she was idly plucking out of the porch were intensely green.

E. M. FORSTER

There is something subversive about this garden. . . a sense of buried things bursting upwards, wordlessly into the light, as if to point, to say: Whatever is silenced will clamor to be heard, though silently.

MARGARET ATWOOD

It's a . . . torture rack, all that budding and pushing, the sap up the tree trunks, the weeds and the insects getting set to fight it out once again, the seeds trying to remember how the hell the DNA is supposed to go, all that competition for a little bit of nitrogen; Christ, it's cruel.

JOHN UPDIKE

Nature does have manure and she does have roots as well as blossoms, and you can't hate the manure and blame the roots for not being blossoms.
BUCKMINSTER FULLER

We are probably all a little cranky in our ideas on manuring. . . . For my part, I cast all my nail parings out of the bathroom window so as to feed the ceanothus below with hoof and horn. Since, at 30 years, this is the oldest ceanothus in my garden, and it is still flourishing, I naturally congratulate myself on a sagacious policy.
CHRISTOPHER LLOYD

"Putting on a little, anyway," of anything handy, particularly fertilizer, I found to be a habit that was hard to break, for like most people starting to garden it seemed to me that if a little was good, more of the same would be better. It isn't.
AMOS PETTINGILL

The sudden shattering of a windowpane made me shudder, that decided it: a vegetable arm, crooked, twisted, in which I had no difficulty recognizing the workings, the surreptitious approach, the reptilian mind of the wisteria, has just struck, broken, and entered.
COLETTE

What hidden virtue is in these things that it is granted to sow themselves with the wind and to grapple the earth with this immitigable stubbornness, and to flourish in spite of obstacles, and never to suffer blight beneath any sun or shade, but always to mock their enemies with the same wicked luxuriance?

NATHANIEL HAWTHORNE

I began to reflect on Nature's eagerness to sow life everywhere, to fill the planet with it, to crowd with it the earth, the air, and the seas. Into every empty corner, into all forgotten things and nooks, Nature struggles to pour life, pouring life into the dead, life into life itself. That immense, overwhelming, relentless, burning ardency of Nature for the stir of life!

HENRY BESTON

Mary, Mary, quite contrary,
How does your garden grow?
With silver bells and cockleshells,
And pretty maids all in a row.

ANONYMOUS NURSERY RHYME

...The earth, genial and indulgent, ever subservient to the wants of man, spreads his walks with flowers, and his table with plenty; returns, with interest, every good committed to her care; ... though constantly teased more to furnish the luxuries of man than his necessities, yet even to the last she continues her kind indulgence, and, when life is over, she piously covers his remains in her bosom.

PLINY THE ELDER

If Nature put not forth her power
About the opening of the flower,
Who is it that could live an hour?

ALFRED TENNYSON

But Nature in her universal procedures is not rational as I am rational when I weed my garden, prune my trees, select my seed or my stock, or arm myself with tools or weapons. In such matters I take a short cut to that which Nature reaches by a slow-roundabout, and wasteful process.

JOHN BURROUGHS

All gardeners need to know when to accept something wonderful and unexpected, taking no credit except for letting it be.

ALLEN LACY

Nature is, above all, profligate. Don't believe them when they tell you how economical and thrifty nature is, whose leaves return to the soil. Wouldn't it be cheaper to leave them on the tree in the first place?

ANNIE DILLARD

In the rain forest these orchids get broken by wind and rain.
They get pollinated randomly and rarely by insects. Their
seedlings are crushed by screaming monkeys. . . . There in
the greenhouse nothing would break the orchids and they
would be pollinated at full moon and high tide by Amado
Vazquez, and their seedlings would be tended in a
sterile box with sterile gloves and sterile tools by Amado
Vazquez's wife, Maria. . . .

JOAN DIDION

Fluffy-ruffle petunias are delicate plants. The seed is as expensive as gold
dust and as fine. It takes weeks to germinate. The seedlings must be
nursed by hand. . . . Once brought months later to maturity, the huge
multi-colored blooms represent beauty flowered into life by the most
desperate of measures.

MARJORIE KINNAN RAWLINGS

In these flats, the soil is mixed fine with coffee grounds and
broken eggshells. Her roses grow dark red and electric on
crushed bones. The tiny heads of lettuce tighten in garters. The
tomato plants droop on thick stems mulched with dried blood
and oak leaves. Asparagus fern and chives blow everyplace like
hair. Mary uses anything around her that's available.

LOUISE ERDRICH

Every rose is an autograph from the hand of God on his world about us. He has inscribed his thoughts in these mysterious hieroglyphics which sense and science have, these many thousand years, been seeking to understand.

THEODORE PARKER

Nature soon takes over if the gardener is absent.

PENELOPE HOBHOUSE

I recall a statement . . . to the effect that the growth of pink clover depended largely on the proximity of old women. The speaker argued that old women kept cats; cats killed mice; mice were prone to destroy the nests of the bumble-bees, which alone were fitted, owing to the length of their probosces, to fertilize the blossoms of the clover. Consequently, a good supply of clover depended on an abundance of old women.

FRANCES T. DANA

But think a moment about a garden forever warm, forever growing, always green, with brilliant dots of color every day of the year—a garden that never rests. There would be no time to plan, no moments to quietly sit and reflect on the triumphs and failures of the preceding seasons, no chance for change.

PETER LOEWER

If a tree dies, plant another in its place.
LINNAEUS

Consider the lilies of the field, how they grow; they neither toil nor spin: yet I tell you, even Solomon in all his glory was not arrayed like one of these.

MATTHEW, 6:28-29

THE FLOWER BED

... Bread feeds the body indeed, but the flowers feed also the soul.
THE KORAN

Is there not a soul beyond utterance, half nymph, half child, in those delicate petals which glow and breathe about the centres of deep colour?

GEORGE ELIOT

The delicate droop of the petals standing out in relief, is like the eyelid of a child.

AUGUSTE RODIN

What a pity flowers can utter no sound!—A singing rose, a whispering violet, a murmuring honeysuckle,—oh, what a rare and exquisite miracle would these be!

HENRY WARD BEECHER

To analyze the charms of flowers is like dissecting music; it is one of those things which it is far better to enjoy, than to attempt fully to understand.

HENRY THEODORE TUCKERMAN

Flowers are restful to look at. They have neither emotions nor conflicts.

SIGMUND FREUD

I perhaps owe having become a painter to flowers.

CLAUDE MONET

To me the meanest flower that blows can give
Thoughts that do often lie too deep for tears.

WILLIAM WORDSWORTH

Deep in their roots,
All flowers keep the light.

THEODORE ROETHKE

For to have complete satisfaction from flowers you must have time to spend with them. There must be rapport. I talk to them and they talk to me.

PRINCESS GRACE OF MONACO

Nothing is too polished to see the beauty of flowers. Nothing too rough to be capable of enjoying them. It attracts, delights all.

DANIEL WEBSTER

What a desolate place would be a world without flowers? It would be a face without a smile; a feast without a welcome.

CLARA L. BALFOUR

As I work among my flowers, I find myself talking to them, reasoning and remonstrating with them, and adoring them as if they were human beings. Much laughter I provoke among my friends by so doing, but that is of no consequence. We are on such good terms, my flowers and I!

CELIA THAXTER

If you sit still and watch, you begin to move with the [crocuses], like moving with the stars, and you feel the sound of their radiance. All the little cells of the flowers must be leaping with flowery life and utterance.

D. H. LAWRENCE

I hunted curious flowers in rapture and muttered thoughts in their praise.
JOHN CLARE

I don't share the opinion of those people who think that people who love flowers are necessarily good. Even those who love animals are not always so; certain people love flowers and animals because they are incapable of getting along with their fellow human beings.
SIGRID UNDSET

I feel certain that almost every American must have a favorite childhood memory of picking flowers—dandelions on a lawn, perhaps, or daisies and buttercups in a meadow, trailing arbutus on a cold New England hillside in spring, a bunch of sweet peas in a hot July garden after admonishments from an adult to cut the stems *long*. . . .
KATHERINE S. WHITE

How curious that the majority of people show their appreciation of a flower's beauty only by selfishly, ignorantly picking every specimen they can find!
NELTJE BLANCHAN

A flower's fragrance declares to all the world that it is fertile, available, and desirable, its sex organs oozing with nectar. Its smell reminds us in vestigial ways of fertility, vigor, life-force, all the optimism, expectancy, and passionate bloom of youth. We inhale its ardent aroma and, no matter what our ages, we feel young and nubile in a world aflame with desire.

DIANE ACKERMAN

Does anything eat flowers? I couldn't recall having seen anything actually eat a flower—are they nature's privileged pets?

ANNIE DILLARD

Oh see how thick the goldcup flowers
Are lying in field and lane,
With dandelions to tell the hours
That never are told again.

A.E. HOUSMAN

The garden, mimic of spring, is gay with flowers. The purple-starred hepatica spreads itself in the sun, and the clustering snow-drops put forth their white heads. . . .

DOROTHY WORDSWORTH

. . . Each beauteous flow'r,
Iris all hues, Roses, and Jessamin
Rear'd high their flourished heads between, and wrought
Mosaic; underfoot the Violet,
Crocus, and Hyacinth with rich inlay
Broider'd the ground, more color'd than with stone
Of costliest Emblem. . . .

JOHN MILTON

Every rose is an autograph from the hand of God on his world
about us. He has inscribed his thoughts in these marvellous
hieroglyphics which sense and science have, these many
thousand years, been seeking to understand.

THEODORE PARKER

Brave flowers, that I could gallant it like you,
And be as little vain;
You come abroad and make a harmless show,
And to your beds of earth again;
You are not proud, you know your birth,
For your embroidered garments are from earth.

HENRY KING

THE KITCHEN GARDEN

The smell of manure, of sun on foliage, of evaporating water, rose to my head; two steps farther, and I could look down into the vegetable garden enclosed within its tall pale of reeds—rich chocolate earth studded emerald green, frothed with the white of cauliflowers, jewelled with the purple globes of eggplant and the scarlet wealth of tomatoes.

DORIS LESSING

Each year the big garden grew smaller and Jane—who grew flowers by choice, not corn or stringbeans—worked at the vegetables more than I did. Each winter I dreamed crops, dreamed marvels of canning . . . and each summer I largely failed. Shamefaced I planted no garden at all.

DONALD HALL

In order to live off a garden, you practically have to live in it.

FRANK MCKINNEY HUBBARD

By the Fourth of July the gardener feels that summer is finally here, and all is well with the world. The tomatoes are looking sturdy, the corn is coming, the beets and carrots are up, and he won't have to buy any plastic salad makings from the supermarket until November.

ROY BARRETTE

I am open to the accusation that I see compost as an end in itself. But we do grow some real red damn tomatoes such as you can't get in the stores. And potatoes, beans, lettuce, collards, onions, squash, cauliflower, eggplant, carrots, peppers. *Dirt* in your own backyard, producing things you eat. Makes you wonder.

ROY BLOUNT, JR.

The trouble is, you cannot grow just one zucchini. Minutes after you plant a single seed, hundreds of zucchini will barge out of the ground and sprawl around the garden, menacing the other vegetables. At night, you will be able to hear the ground quake as more and more zucchinis erupt.

DAVE BARRY

The cauliflower. . . emerged as a fragrant little head in the vegetable garden, a bumpy vegetable brain that looked innocent and edible enough. . . . I would go to the vegetable patch and squat over the cauliflowers as they came out one by one, hold them between my knees, and chew as many craters as I could into their jaunty tightness.

SARA SULERI

Nature made the carrot, but man modified it, planted it, grew it. There are two wills in collaboration here—the will of the carrot to be orange and to taste carroty and so forth—and the will of human beings to have it be a large carrot that travels well, keeps in cold storage, and so forth.

NOEL PERRIN

The crooked little tomato branches, pulpy and pale as if made of cheap green paper, broke under the weight of so much fruit; there was something frantic in such fertility, a crying-out like that of children frantic to please.

JOHN UPDIKE

...We will gladly send the management a jar of our wife's green-tomato pickle from last summer's crop—dark green, spicy, delicious, costlier than pearls when you figure the overhead.

E. B. WHITE

Last night, we had three small zucchini for dinner that were grown within fifty feet of our back door. I estimate they cost somewhere in the neighborhood of $371.49 each.

ANDY ROONEY

It is quite true that eggplants next to potatoes will be more attractive to the potato beetle than the potatoes are: that zinnias (especially in white or pale colors), white roses and white geraniums will lure Japanese beetles away from other plants; and that dill charms the tomato hornworm into deserting the tomatoes. What of it? What of the eggplants, zinnias, white roses, dill, I have lost in the process?

ELEANOR PERÉNYI

To get the best results you must talk to your vegetables.

CHARLES, PRINCE OF WALES

The garden cost Amelia no end of work and worry; she tended the delicate tomato vines as though they were newborn infants, and suffered momentary sinking of the heart whenever she detected signs of weakness in any of the hardier vegetables. She was grateful for the toil in which she could dwell as a sort of refuge from deeper thought.

MARTHA OSTENSO

I came to love my rows, my beans, though so many more than I wanted. They attached me to the earth, and so I got strength like Antaeus.

HENRY DAVID THOREAU

When Bertha Ingqvist, David's mother, said one April, "I don't believe I'll put in a garden this year," they knew she didn't have long. When you no longer care about fresh tomatoes and sweet corn, then death is near, and so she died the first week of June and now she is enriching the soil up there on the hill.

GARRISON KEILLOR

I want death to find me planting my cabbages.

MICHEL EYQUIEM DE MONTAIGNE

. . . Herbs are of two sorts, therefore it is meet that we have two gardens: a garden for flowers and a kitchen garden.

WILLIAM LAWSON

Gardening with herbs, which is becoming increasingly popular, is indulged in by those who like subtlety in their plants in preference to brilliance.

HELEN MORGENTHAU FOX

Morris dancing still lingers but, on the whole, we have taken the olde-tyme merriness out of the countryside. About time too, and as a gardener, not a cook, I feel the same about most herb gardens. . . For gardeners, herbs mean hard work, frequent renewal and, usually, a patch of unkempt ugliness.

ROBIN LANE FOX

I plant Rosemary all over the garden, so pleasant is it to know that at every few steps one may draw the kindly branchlets through one's hand, and have the enjoyment of their incomparable incense; and I grow it against walls, so that the sun may draw out its inexhaustible sweetness to greet me as I pass. . . .

GERTRUDE JEKYLL

My friend first points out on one side the beds of basil, burnet, chives, but as she turns to the other side her eyes sparkle with a happy light. For this is her tussie-mussie garden, mignonette, rosemary, lemon verbena . . . all of the old-time favorites. Each plant is a personality, each kind of herb a fragrant memory for any visitor to the garden.

ROSETTA E. CLARKSON

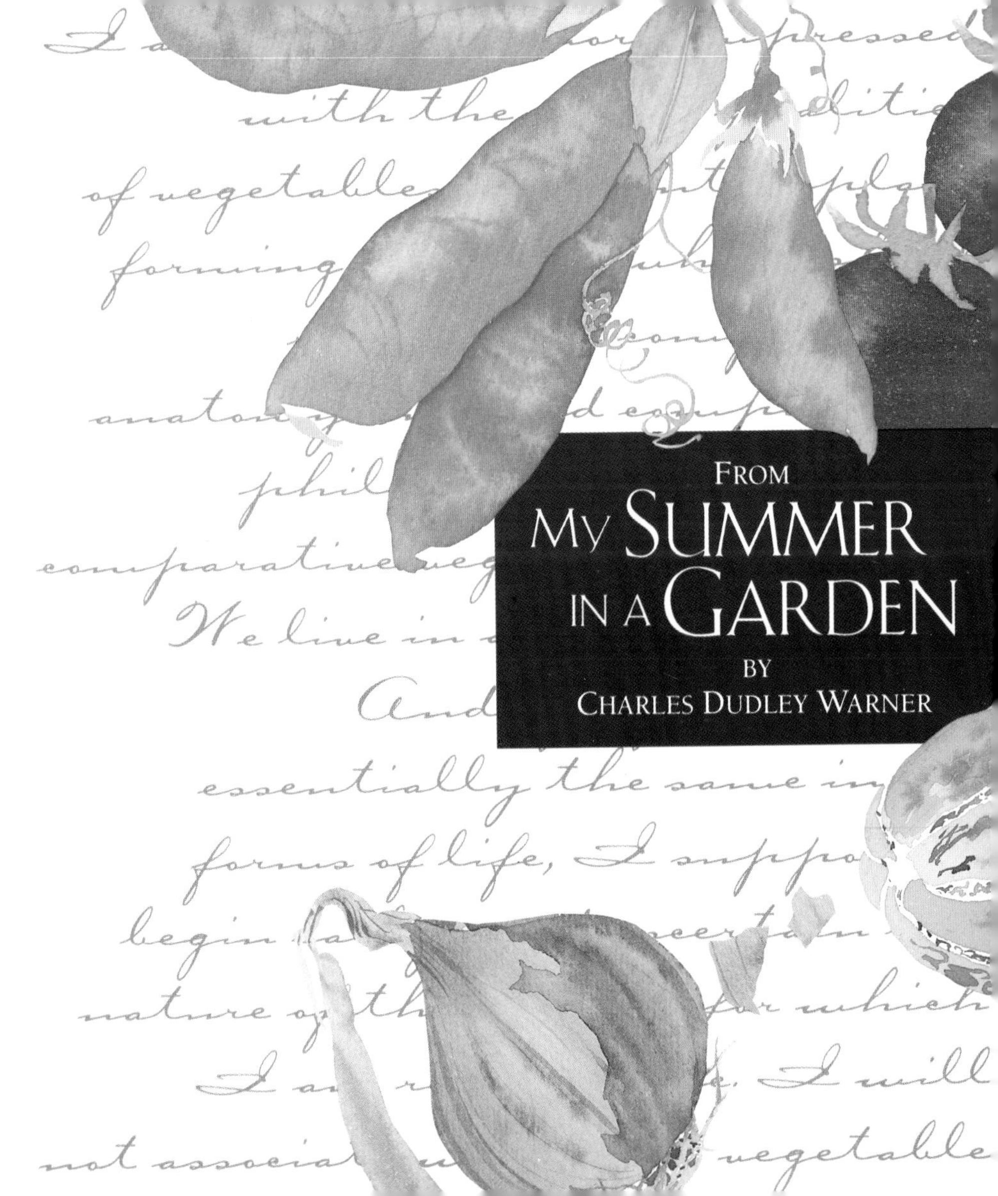

From

My Summer in a Garden

by

Charles Dudley Warner

I AM MORE AND MORE IMPRESSED

with the moral qualities of vegetables, and contemplate forming a science which shall rank with comparative anatomy and comparative philology,—the science of comparative vegetable morality. We live in a age of protoplasm. And, if life-matter is essentially the same in all forms of life, I suppose to begin early, and ascertain the nature of the plants for which I am responsible. I will not associate with any vegetable which is disreputable, or has not some quality that can contribute to my moral growth. I do not care to be seen much with the squashes or the dead-beets. Fortunately I can cut down any sorts I do not like with the hoe. . . .

Why do we respect some vegetables, and despise others, when all of them come to an equal honor or ignominy on the table? The bean is a graceful, confiding, engaging vine; but you never can put beans into poetry, nor into the highest sort of prose. There is no dignity in the bean. Corn, which, in my garden, grows alongside the bean, and, so far as I can see, with no affectation of superiority, is, however, the child of song. It waves in all literature. But mix it with beans, and its high tone is gone.

Succotash is vulgar. It is the bean in it. The bean is a vulgar vegetable, without culture, or any flavor of high society among vegetables. Then there is the cool cucumber, like so many people,—good for nothing when it is ripe and the wildness has gone out of it. How inferior in quality it is to the melon, which grows upon a similar vine, is of a like watery consistency, but is not half so valuable! The cucumber is a sort of low comedian in a company where the melon is a minor gentleman. I might also contrast the celery with the potato. The associations are as opposite as the dining-room of the duchess and the cabin of the peasant. I admire the potato, both in vine and blossom; but it is not aristocratic. I began digging my potatoes, by the way, about the 4th of July; and I fancy I have discovered the right way to do it. I treat the potato just as I would a cow. I do not pull them up, and shake them out, and destroy them; but I dig carefully at the side of the hill, remove the fruit which is grown, leaving the vine undisturbed: and my theory is, that it will go on bearing, and submitting to my exactions, until the frost cuts it down. It is a game that one would not undertake with a vegetable of tone.

The lettuce is to me a most interesting study. Lettuce is like conversation: it must be fresh and crisp, so sparkling, that you scarcely notice the bitter in it. Lettuce, like most talkers, is, however, apt to run rapidly to seed. Blessed is that sort which comes to a head, and so remains, like a few people I know; growing more solid and satisfactory and tender at the same time, and whiter at the centre, and crisp in their maturity. . . . I feel that I am in the best society when I am with lettuce. It is in the select circle of vegetables. The tomato appears well on the table; but you do not want to ask its origin. It is a most agreeable parvenu. Of course, I have said nothing about the berries. They live in another and more ideal region; except, perhaps, the currant. Here we see, that, even among berries, there are degrees of breeding. The currant is well enough, clear as truth, and exquisite in color; but I ask you to notice how far it is from the exclusive hauteur of the aristocratic strawberry, and the native refinement of the quietly elegant raspberry.

I do not know that chemistry, searching for protoplasm, is able to discover the tendency of vegetables. It can only be found by outward observation. I confess that I am suspicious of the bean, for instance. There are signs in it of an unregulated life. I put up the most attractive sort of poles for my Limas. They stand high and straight, like church-spires, in my theological garden,—lifted up; and some of them have even budded like Aaron's rod. No church-steeple in a New England village was ever better fitted to draw to it the rising generation on Sunday, than those poles to lift up my beans toward heaven. Some of them did run up the sticks seven feet, and then straggled off into the air in a wanton manner; but more than half of them went galivanting off to the neighboring grape-trellis, and wound their tendrils with the tendrils of the grape, with a disregard of the proprieties of life which is a satire upon human nature. And the grape is morally no better. I think the ancients, who were not troubled with the recondite mystery of protoplasm, were right in the mythic union of Bacchus and Venus.

Talk about the Darwinian theory of development, and the principle of natural selection! I should like to see a garden let to run in accordance with it. If I had left my vegetables and weeds to a free fight, in which the strongest specimens only should come to maturity, and the weaker go to the wall, I can clearly see that I should have had a pretty mess of it. It would have been a scene of passion and license and brutality. The "pusley" would have strangled the strawberry; the upright corn, which has now ears to hear the guilty beating of the hearts of the children who steal the raspberries, would have been dragged to the earth by the wandering bean; the snake-grass would have left no place for the potatoes under ground; and the tomatoes would have been swamped by the lusty weeds. With a firm hand, I have had to make my own "natural selection."

THE ORCHARD

Now I am in the garden at the back . . . a very preserve of butterflies, as I remember it, with a high fence, and a gate and padlock; where the fruit clusters on the trees, riper and richer than fruit has ever been since, in any other garden, and where my mother gathers some in a basket, while I stand by, bolting furtive gooseberries, and trying to look unmoved.

CHARLES DICKENS

In an orchard there should be enough to eat, enough to lay up, enough to be stolen, and enough to rot upon the ground.

JAMES BOSWELL

The odors of fruits waft me to my southern home, to my childhood frolics in the peach orchard.

HELEN KELLER

Hark, where my blossomed pear-tree in the hedge
Leans to the field and scatters on the clover
Blossoms and dewdrops—at the bent spray's edge. . . .

ROBERT BROWNING

She had only to stand in the orchard, to put her hand on a little crab tree and look up at the apples, to make you feel the goodness of planting and tending and harvesting at last.

WILLA CATHER

Tall thriving Trees confessed the fruitful Mold;
The reddening Apple ripens here to Gold,
Here the blue Fig with luscious Juice o'erflows,
With deeper Red the full Pomegranate glows
The Branch here bends beneath the weighty Pear,
And verdant Olives flourish round the Year.

HOMER

Newton sat in an orchard, and an apple, plumping down on his head, started a train of thought which opened the heavens to us. Had it been in California, the size of the apples there would have saved him the trouble of much thinking thereafter, perhaps, opening the heavens to him, and not to us.

HENRY WARD BEECHER

Oh, give us pleasure in the orchard white,
Like nothing else by day, like ghosts by night.

ROBERT FROST

. . . The dew falls on the wind-
Milled dust of the apple tree and. . . the winged
             Apple seed glides,
And falls, and flowers. . . .
DYLAN THOMAS

A seed hidden in the heart of an apple is an orchard invisible.
WELSH PROVERB

TREES, GRASS, AND GREENERY

A garden without trees scarcely deserves to be called a garden.
HENRY ELLACOMBE

But under the beaming, constant and almost vertical sun of
Virginia, shade is our Elysium. In the absence of this no beauty
of the eye can be enjoyed.
THOMAS JEFFERSON

There are those who say that trees shade the garden too much, and
interfere with the growth of the vegetables. There may be something in
this: but when I go down the potato rows, the rays of the sun glancing

upon my shining blade, the sweat pouring from my face, I should be grateful for shade.

CHARLES DUDLEY WARNER

It is hard to explain to the modern garden-lover, whose whole conception of the charm of gardens is formed of successive pictures of flower-loveliness, how [the Italian villa garden's] effect of enchantment can be produced by anything so dull and monotonous as a mere combination of clipped green and stone-work.

EDITH WHARTON

People in suburbia see trees differently than foresters do. They cherish every one. It is useless to speak of the probability that a certain tree will die when the tree is in someone's backyard. . . . You are talking about a personal asset, a friend, a monument, not about board feet of lumber.

ROGER SWAIN

. . . Bread and butter, devoid of charm in the drawing-room, is ambrosia eaten under a tree.

ELIZABETH VON ANTRIM

Those beeches and smooth limes—there was something enervating in the very sight of them; but the strong knotted old oaks had no bending languor in them—the sight of them would give a man some energy.

GEORGE ELIOT

. . . Evolution did not intend trees to grow singly. Far more than ourselves they are social creatures, and no more natural as isolated specimens than man is as a marooned sailor or hermit.

JOHN FOWLES

To be able to walk *under* the branches of a tree that you have planted is really to feel you have arrived with your garden. So far we are on the way: we can now stand beside ours.

MIRABEL OSLER

. . . For the birches had infused into us some of their own suppleness and strength.

JOHN BURROUGHS

The wonder is that we can see these trees and not wonder more.

RALPH WALDO EMERSON

The ash is most beautiful in the forest, the pine in the garden, the poplar by the river, the fir on the mountain heights. . . .

VIRGIL

Of all the wonders of nature, a tree in summer is perhaps the most remarkable, with the possible exception of a moose singing "Embraceable You" in spats.

WOODY ALLEN

The apple-bloom—it is falling fast now as the days advance—who can count the myriad blossoms of the orchard? There are leaves upon the hedges which bound that single meadow. . . enough to occupy the whole summer to count; and before it was half done they would be falling. But that half would be enough for shadow—for use . . . There is no *enough* in nature. It is one vast prodigality.

RICHARD JEFFERIES

They walked over the crackling leaves in the garden, between the lines of Box, breathing its fragrance of eternity; for this is one of the odors which carry us out of time into the abysses of the unbeginning past; if we ever lived on another ball of stone than this, it must be that there was Box growing on it.

OLIVER WENDELL HOLMES

Birth, life, and death—each took place on the hidden side of a leaf.

TONI MORRISON

He saw grasses. . . . They were varied kinds: fescues, rye grass, couch grass, meadow grass, hair grass, silky bent and quaking grass. They were silver-green, green-gold, pale and glassy, clear, new elm-leaf green and darker, bitter marshy-green. Fine lines down their stems glistened like stretched hairs: their finely swollen joints were glossy and shiny. . . . they seemed almost impossible in their intricacy and difference one from another. Also beautiful.

A. S. BYATT

The grasses become braille as I run my fingers through them.
TERRY TEMPEST WILLIAMS

. . . We love most the soft turf which, beneath the flickering shadows of scattered trees, is thrown like a smooth natural carpet over the swelling outline of the smiling earth. Grass, not grown into tall meadows, or wild bog tussocks, but softened and refined by the frequent touches of the patient mower, till at last it becomes a perfect wonder of tufted freshness and verdure.

ANDREW JACKSON DOWNING

Whoever spends the early hours of one summer, while the dew spangles the grass, in pushing these grass-cutters over a velvety lawn, breathing the fresh sweetness of the morning air and the perfume of new mown hay, will never rest contented again in the city.

FRANK SCOTT

Any sensible person with a home would pay grass not to grow if it would take the money, but instead most of us encourage it to get longer. Just when it reaches a nice height we cut it off so it looks like as Marine drill sergeant's haircut.

ANDY ROONEY

"Why, one can hear and see the grass growing!" thought Levin, noticing a wet, slate-colored aspen leaf moving beside a blade of young grass.

LEO TOLSTOY

A grass-blade's no easier to make than an oak.
JAMES RUSSELL LOWELL

Grass is the forgiveness of nature—her constant benediction. Forests decay, harvests perish, flowers vanish, but grass is immortal.
BRIAN INGALLS

VASES, POTS, AND GREENHOUSES

The pleasure of picking a few flowers and finding the right vase for them is incomparable.
MAY SARTON

Belovéd, thou hast brought me many flowers
Plucked in the garden, all the summer through
And winter, and it seemed as if they grew
In this close room, nor missed the sun and showers.
ELIZABETH BARRETT BROWNING

As a child I remember long wands of various flowering bushes being brought indoors at this time of year. They were put in large dramatic groups in big vases in the icy front hall where sooner or later they got knocked over by my father. His outraged shouts about "your mother's confounded sticks" is a very early memory.

THALASSA CRUSSO

Charles is not much interested in flowers, but he has, partly through Liz's influence, become accustomed to them, both indoors and out. His own flat, where he lives alone, is flowerless. Sometimes he buys himself a bunch of daffodils and shoves them in a jug, but they never look convincing.

MARGARET DRABBLE

... And from him I received all of earth's gifts. I always had the privilege of the first violets he had gathered under the dry leaves, the first strawberries from the garden, the first cherries. For my bedside table, he brought the first roses. . . .

ÉMILIE CARLES

Barbie had kept the roses in her bedroom all night; young buds, because she had wanted them to begin to unfold and absorb the substance of her dreams and waking meditations....

PAUL SCOTT

Indoors it so happened that a Christmas cactus had chosen this moment to bloom. Its lush blossoms, fuchsia-shaped but pure red rather than magenta, hung at the drooping ends of strange, thick stems and outlined themselves in blood against the glistening background of the frosty pane—jungle flower against frostflower. . . .

JOSEPH WOOD KRUTCH

No one pulls the shades at night, not because modesty has been forgotten, but because shade pulling has become both impossible and unnecessary—so dense are the flowerpots on the windowsills, so thick are the leaves against the glass.

ROGER SWAIN

And these [house]plants are much like the Vietnam War—once you have invested enough labor and woe, you are strangely unwilling to acknowledge that it was a stupid mistake to begin with. You just go on and on.

HENRY MITCHELL

I have no plants in my house. They won't live for me. Some of them don't even wait to die, they commit suicide.

JERRY SEINFELD

Who loves a garden loves a greenhouse too.

WILLIAM COWPER

When I was nine I would deliberately miss the school bus in order to walk home, because by walking I could pass a greenhouse. I recall being told at that particular greenhouse that the purchase of a nickel pansy did not entitle me to "spend the day," and at another that my breathing was "using up the air."

JOAN DIDION

All next morning from sunrise to the noon she worked in the greenhouse. What to do and where to start? Clean out the jungle. Start in the corner near the door, which as soon as the sun hit it began to smell of florist damp and root reek and rain forest.

WALKER PERCY

I managed then to keep a few square yards on a shelf for staging in an unheated greenhouse, and those few square yards were crowded with tiny bright things from New Year's Day to Easter. Their brilliance contrasted with the snow and the leaden skies; it was like coming into an aviary of tropical birds or butterflies. . . .

VITA SACKVILLE-WEST

All day and every day
(my pet hummingbird) haunts
the garden, and when tired rests
contentedly on the small twig
of a dry pea-stick near the
Larkspurs. The tiny less
blossom about h

Hollyhock flo

glowing pink

there all day and out of the

h

and wheel

one comes

p start

beauty and he

FROM
AN ISLAND GARDEN
BY
CELIA THAXTER

ALL DAY AND EVERYDAY [my pet hummingbird] haunts the garden, and when tired rests contentedly on the small twig of a dry pea-stick near the Larkspurs. The rosy Peas blossom about him, the Hollyhock flowers unfold in glowing pink with lace-like edges of white; the bees hum there all day in and out of the many flowers; the butterflies hover and waver and wheel. When one comes too near him, up starts my beauty and chases him away on burnished wings, away beyond the garden's bounds, and returns to occupy his perch in triumph,—the dry twig he has taken for his home the whole sweet summer long. Other humming-birds haunt the place, but he belongs there; they go and come, but he keeps to his perch and his Larkspurs faithfully. He is so tame he never stirs from his twig for anybody, no matter how near a person may come; he alights on my arms and hands and hair unafraid; he rifles the flowers I hold, when I am gathering them, and I sometimes think he is the very most charming thing in the garden. The jealous bees and the butterflies follow the flowers I carry also, sometimes all the way into the house. The other day, as I sat in the piazza which the vines shade with their broad green leaves and sweet white flowers climbing up to the eaves and over the roof, I saw the humming-birds hovering over the whole expanse of green, to and fro, and discovered that they were picking off and devouring the large transparent aphides scattered, I am happy to say but sparingly, over its surface, every little gnat and midge they snapped up with avidity. I had fancied they lived on honey, but they appeared to like the insects quite as well. . . .

The summer life in the garden of the winged things of the air is most charming,—the wonderful creatures that have escaped, as it were, from the earth. The life that crawls and creeps and devours and destroys, in the forms of slug and cutworm and all hideous shapes, is utterly forgotten as we watch these ethereal beings, fluttering, quivering, darting, dancing, wavering, wheeling, rejoicing aloft in merry flight. The Larkspur spikes bend with the weight of the booming bees, the whole blossoming space is alive with many-colored butterflies like floating flowers, and the hummingbirds are a perpetual pleasure. They are astir even before sunrise, when the air is yet chill with the breath of the retreating night,— there they are, vibrating with their soft humming over the Larkspur blossoms which are themselves like exquisite azure birds all posed for flight, or diving deep into the fragrant trumpets of the Honeysuckle, every where flashing in emerald and ruby as the sun's first beams strike them, like the living jewels they are. Their fearlessness is something amazing. I shall never forget the surprise of joy that filled me when for the first time one alighted on my sleeve and rested, as much at home as if I were a stick or a harmless twig! Sparrows and nuthatches had often alighted on my head as I stood musing over my flowers, perfectly still, but to have this tiny spark of brilliant life come to anchor, as it were, on anything so earthly as my arm was indeed a nine days' wonder! Now it has grown to be an old story, but it is never any less delightful.

August 18th. This morning the garden was so dry again that when I sought it at sunrise, in spite of the heavy dew, I took the hose and turned on the water, showering the place most thoroughly. When I had done the drops clung thickly to everything, to the sprays of Sweet Peas especially, the rough surfaces of their leaves and stalks catching and holding the water more tenaciously than the smoother foliage; they were begemmed, as it were, with so many sparkling spheres of light. The tamest, dearest hummingbird, whose home is in the Larkspurs, was greatly excited by this unexpected and refreshing shower, and whirred about me, uttering continually his one fine, sweet, keen note. When my rain-storm ceased he flew to the Sweet Peas close to his azure bower, and sitting on a green spray already bent with the weight of the clear drops, proceeded to take his morning bath with the most cheerful enjoyment. He fluttered his tiny wings and ducked his head and wagged his tail and drenched himself completely; his feathers were so soaking wet that his little body looked no bigger than a bumblebee; then he flew up and lighted on the tallest pea-stick that reached over the fence among the Larkspurs: there sitting on his favorite twig he rapidly preened his feathers, shook himself, spread his wings and tail and combed them with his slender beak and dried them in the broad, bright beams that poured across the garden in the low sun. With claws and beak he smoothed and arranged his dainty raiment, perfectly regardless of me, his ardent admirer, standing near enough to touch him with my finger. Then he fluttered in and out among the flowers, dipping into every dewy chalice and feasting on his fragrant honey.

THE BIRDS AND THE BEES

She was stretched on her back beneath the pear tree soaking in the alto chant of the visiting bees, the gold of the sun and the panting breath of the breeze when the inaudible voice of it all came to her. She saw a dust-bearing bee sink into the sanctum of a bloom; the thousand sister-calyxes arch to meet the love embrace and the ecstatic shiver of the tree from root to tiniest branch creaming in every blossom and frothing with delight.

ZORA NEALE HURSTON

> . . . I knew the birds
> and insects, which looked fathered by the flowers . . .
> butterflies, that bear
> Upon their blue wings such red embers round
> They seem to scorch the blue air into holes
> Each flight they take. . . .

ELIZABETH BARRETT BROWNING

Flowers set their caps for passing bees, appealing to every instinct and appetite—sensory, dietetic and comfort. They hung out banners and flags of the favorite colors of the insects; they shamelessly sprayed the air with alluring perfumes, and spread buffet luncheons with nutritious and sweet nectar. The susceptible bee alighted on the colored carpet of welcome, and found a wide, easy way to the banquet.

WILLIAM BEEBE

The bees like plum-blossoms, and so do I. They smell exactly like cherry Lifesavers taste.

SUE HUBBELL

The honey-bee's great ambition is to be rich, to lay up great stores, to possess the sweet of every flower that blooms. She is more than provident. Enough will not satisfy her; she must have all she can get by hook or by crook.

JOHN BURROUGHS

. . . The exquisite butterflies, gentle creatures full of life and beauty who stalk nothing and live on nectar, like the gods of old.

DIANE ACKERMAN

There was a Bower at the further end, with honeysuckle, jessamine, and creeping plants—one of those sweet retreats, which humane men erect for the accommodation of spiders.

CHARLES DICKENS

Also you could make the acquaintance of strange, busy insect things running about on various unknown but evidently serious errands, sometimes carrying tiny scraps of straw or feather or food, or climbing blades of grass as if they were trees from whose tops one could look out to explore the country.

FRANCES HODGSON BURNETT

She sat down in a weed patch, her elbows on her knees, and kept her eyes on the small, mysterious world of the ground. In the shade and sun of grass blade forests, small living things had their metropolis.

NANCY PRICE

Gardeners and farmers express their detestation of worms; the former because they render their walks unsightly, and make them much work: and the latter because, as they think, worms eat their green corn. But these men would find that the earth without worms would soon become cold, hard-bound, and void of fermentation; and consequently sterile. . . .

GILBERT WHITE

The sparrows may perhaps vex you by nibbling your crocuses, and the blackbirds may steal your cherries; but remember they cannot trouble you in this sort of way all the year round. They will be gobbling up snails and caterpillars and butterflies in the dewy dawn, when you perhaps are sleeping and unhappily unconscious of the benefactions of your feathered friends.

JAMES SHIRLEY HIBBERD

I once had a sparrow alight upon my shoulder for a moment while I was hoeing in a village garden, and I felt that I was more distinguished by that circumstance than I should have been by any epaulet I could have worn.

HENRY DAVID THOREAU

I value my garden more for being full of blackbirds than of cherries, and very frankly give them fruit for their songs.

JOSEPH ADDISON

THE CHALLENGE OF THE GARDEN

Gardening is a humbling experience.

MARTHA STEWART

No garden is without its weeds.

THOMAS FULLER

Scents and strawberries are not the sole marvels of a summer garden: weeds are there too, sprouting in impossible places, multiplying in a month's absence and never leaving flowerbeds alone.

ROBIN LANE FOX

Crabgrass can grow on bowling balls in airless rooms, and there is no known way to kill it that does not involve nuclear weapons.

DAVE BARRY

Most of these forward weeds are of sorts that do not survive having their heads cut off half a dozen times; while good lawn grasses fairly laugh and grow fat with decapitation. Weeds of certain species, however, will persist in thrusting their uninvited heads through the best kept lawns. These are to be dealt with like cancers. A long sharp knife, and busy fingers, are the only cure for them.

FRANK SCOTT

... On no other ground
Can I sow my seed
Without tearing up
Some stinking weed.

WILLIAM BLAKE

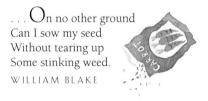

When the delicate flowers of the wild carrot are still unsoiled by the dust from the highway, and fresh from the early summer rains, they are very beautiful, adding much to the appearance of the roadsides and fields along which they grow so abundantly as to strike despair into the heart of the farmer, for this is, perhaps, the "peskiest" of all the weeds with which he has to contend.

FRANCES T. DANA

She loved everything that grew in God's earth, even the weeds. With one exception. If she found a blade of nut grass in her yard it was like the Second Battle of the Marne. . . .

HARPER LEE

The Dandelion's pallid tube
Astonishes the Grass,—
And Winter instantly becomes
An infinite Alas.

EMILY DICKINSON

Now 'tis the spring, and weeds are shallow-rooted;
Suffer them now and they'll o'ergrow the garden.

WILLIAM SHAKESPEARE

Almost all the horticultural nuisances that make grass growing such a
problem in this country are foreigners. The pestilential ground ivy is an
Asiatic, while couch grass, crab grass, shepherd's-purse, dandelions,
docks, and plantains are all European imports. Just think of the
unblemished velvety smoothness of our lawns if we could but
deport all these particular weeds!

THALASSA CRUSSO

The haughty thistle o'er all danger towers,
In every place the very wasp of flowers.

JOHN CLARE

But make no mistake: the weeds will win: nature bats last.

ROBERT MICHAEL PYLE

What is a weed? A plant whose virtues have not yet been discovered.
RALPH WALDO EMERSON

All gardeners know the trouble we have with some insects, and few are more provoking than the striped bug on the young Melon vines. Place one of your pet Toads (and all gardeners should have such pets) among these vines, and watch him. See how like a streak of lightning that tongue flashes out, and how the Melon Bug flashes in.
ISAAC TRIMBLE

Early in April, as I was vigorously hoeing in a corner, I unearthed a huge toad, to my perfect delight and satisfaction; he had lived all winter, he had doubtless fed on slugs all the autumn. I could have kissed him on the spot!
CELIA THAXTER

Now, here in the Northwest, venomous snakes are not everyday fare, but another sinister and slimy character lurks beneath every leaf, waiting to attack the unsuspecting gardener. Anybody who has ever stepped barefoot on a large and squashy slug will immediately see both the charm and the application of this concept. Slug Boots. I like it.
ANN LOVEJOY

Or perhaps you notice a congregation of ladybugs on a rose stalk. Don't invoke the old nursery saying and ask them to fly away home. Their house is not on fire. Your roses are, with aphids, which the ladybugs are feeding on—and you can bless yourself that they have come to your rescue.

ELEANOR PERÉNYI

The garden air is full of the sound of crickets, the year's clock made audible, ticking off the days. I have learned that it is the black field crickets that have eaten my tomatoes in late summer, but there is still such a red flood ripening on the window sills that I do not begrudge them what they take now.

ROBERT FINCH

But in your generation and mine, men must shoulder their squirt-guns [filled with insecticides] as our ancestors shouldered their muskets, and see only the promise of time when they shall be beaten into pruning-hooks and plowshares and there shall come the peace of a silent warfare!

LIBERTY HYDE BAILEY

Immunized early against the chemical quick fix, when I came into a garden and an appreciable pest population of my own a few years back, I declared this small, urbane patch of green a pesticide-free zone—a safe haven to birds, butterflies, fireflies, dragonflies, worms, not to mention aphids, leafhoppers, mites, scale, mealybugs.

One season of natural free-for-all took me from organic pacifism to biological war.

PATTI HAGAN

And although I don't for a minute imagine that my ninety-eight-cent can of poison spray will annihilate a whole species of insect and thereby throw what the ecologists call "the totality of interrelationships" out of kilter, I do worry that I might kill villains and heroes indiscriminately, repay the kindness of my invaluable friends, the birds, with a case of acute gastritis and possible even jeopardize the health and well-being of those great gardening assistants, my grandchildren.

CELESTINE SIBLEY

To a coon, six feet of wire fence is merely a jungle gym upon which it can work up an appetite before raiding the corn.

ROY BARRETTE

[The trespassing pig] pranced to the front yard and gave himself with abandon to my fourth planting of fluffy-ruffle petunias. I arose as one in a trance, picked up my gun, stepped to the petunia bed and shot him dead where he fed. . . . The roast pork was perfection. The meat was as white as the skimmed milk and the petunia roots on which it had been fattened.

MARJORIE KINNAN RAWLINGS

The great wonder, in gardening, is that so many plants live.

CHRISTOPHER LLOYD

I should never have done, were I to recount to you all the inconveniences and accidents which the grains of our fields, the trees of our orchards, as well as those of the woods, are exposed to. If bountiful Nature is kind to us on the one hand, on the other she wills that we shall purchase her kindness not only with sweats and labour but with vigilance and care.

HECTOR ST. JOHN DE CRÈVECOEUR

The principal value of a garden is not understood. It is not to give the possessors vegetables and fruit (that can be better and cheaper done by the market-gardeners), but to teach him patience and philosophy, and the higher virtues,—hope deferred, and expectations blighted, leading directly to resignation, and sometimes to alienation.

CHARLES DUDLEY WARNER

If you grow a garden you are going to shed some sweat, and you are going to spend some time bent over; you will experience some aches and pains. But it is in the willingness to accept this discomfort that we strike the most telling blow against the power plants and what they represent.

WENDELL BERRY

It was difficult to enjoy the trees and flowers when I was so aware of all that I had not yet done—pruning, weeding, transplanting, mulching, composting, tagging. When I was doing the work myself, I was happy, free.

JAY NEUGEBOREN

The roses had given up their annual struggle to keep things cheerful and now hemmed in Mr. Rowse's path with thorns.

FAY WELDON

Now the gardener is the one who has seen everything ruined so many times that (even as his pain increases with each loss) he comprehends—truly knows—that where there was a garden once, it can be again, or where there never was, there yet can be a garden. . . .

HENRY MITCHELL

Alas, how seldom do these little schemes come off. Something will go wrong; some puppy will bury a bone; some mouse will eat the bulbs; some mole will heave the daphnes and the lilac out of the ground.

Still, no gardener would be a gardener if he did not live in hope.

VITA SACKVILLE-WEST

What though his phlox and hollyhocks ere half a month demised? What though his ampelopsis clambered not as advertised? Though every seed was guaranteed and every standard true— Forget, forgive they did not live! Believe, and buy anew!

RUDYARD KIPLING

GARDEN DESIGN

To make a great garden, one must have a great idea or a great opportunity.

SIR GEORGE SITWELL

Gardeners work with an ever-receding ideal of perfection: no sooner is something growing well than they see how to place it better or give it a better neighbour. To other's eyes, all may look as well as could be expected, but a good gardener's eye sees more to be improved.

ROBIN LANE FOX

In garden arrangement, as in all other kinds of decorative work, one has not only to acquire a knowledge of what to do, but also to gain some wisdom in perceiving what it is well to let alone.

GERTRUDE JEKYLL

Almost any one may succeed in laying out and planting a garden in right lines, and may give it an air of stateliness and grandeur, by costly decorations; and even now, there are perhaps thousands who would express greater delight in walking through such a garden, than in surveying one where the finest natural beauties are combined.

ANDREW JACKSON DOWNING

She doesn't care for delicate blooms, she goes for the gorgeous Las Vegas-floor show-type flowers. Tiger lilies, asters, and dahlias. Flowers that sag under the weight of their fabulous hats. Big American Beauties and giant mums that when you see them you can almost hear the Casa Loma orchestra. The yard movement in Lake Wobegon has been toward the activity yard, but Mrs. Schwab carries on the old show-yard tradition.

GARRISON KEILLOR

In order to comprehend the beauty of a Japanese garden, it is necessary to understand—or at least to learn to understand—the beauty of stone.

LAFCADIO HEARN

Almost any plant will live for a season or so in a spoonful of mould, if watered twice a day, and watched like a criminal at large; but if plants are to thrive in a rockery, they must be encouraged to strike their roots deep into a soil adapted to their nature. . . .

JAMES SHIRLEY HIBBERD

My ballet work influenced me a lot [in designing my garden]. I was repeating my thoughts with the plants. I put them like the dancers into what I thought the right places and then moved them about.

FREDERICK ASHTON

There are many ways of spending one's money in gardening but the most tempting, at least to me, occurs with the arrival of the bulb catalogues. Bulbs seem to cry out to be planted in quantities and it is hard to remain deaf to their cries.

CHRISTOPHER LLOYD

The mere fact that you get a lot of seeds in a packet doesn't mean you have to plant all of them.

HENRY MITCHELL

He wondered if I had heard of perennials. Of course I had heard of perennials. Every Sunday the news in the papers waited until I had finished the garden sections; I subscribed to four garden magazines; I now owned six garden books—how could I have kept from hearing about perennials? But that I knew nothing about growing perennials was obvious to Mr. Platt.

AMOS PETTINGILL

Perennials can be moved! Many of them have traveled long distances in our own garden. Had they belonged to an airline travel club, I am sure a few would have won a trip to Hawaii by now.

FREDERICK MCGOURTY

A woman's log cabin should be her castle and she should feel free, even comfortable, to have a lawn, mown or unmown, a weed patch or a jungle, if it suits her.

CELESTINE SIBLEY

That's what I should have done instead of transplanting phlox. Their roots were tough, and I could never find the proper place to put them, the proper fence to set them off. White phlox up against a white fence, it never worked. I should have painted the fence blue.

LOUISE ERDRICH

There is no "The End" to be written, neither can you, like an architect, engrave in stone the day the garden was finished; a painter can frame his picture, a composer notate his coda, but a garden is always on the move.

MIRABEL OSLER

IN ALL KINDS OF WEATHER

Weather means more when you have a garden. There's nothing like listening to a shower and thinking how it is soaking in and around your lettuce and green beans.

HENRY VAN DYKE

Every year it seems to me I hear complaints about spring. It is either "late" or "unusually cold," "abnormally dry" or "fantastically wet," for no one is ever willing to admit that there is no such thing as a normal spring.

THALASSA CRUSSO

The thirsty Earth soaks up the rain,
And drinks, and gapes for drink again.
The plants suck in the earth, and are
With constant drinking fresh and fair.

ABRAHAM COWLEY

Day after day we looked for rain, and day after day we saw nothing but the sun. Lavender that we had planted in the spring died. The patch of grass in front of the house abandoned its ambitions to become a lawn and turned into the dirty yellow of poor straw. The earth shrank, revealing its knuckles and bones, rocks and roots that had been invisible before.

PETER MAYLE

Thou visitest the earth and waterest it. . . .
Thou waterest its furrows abundantly,
settling its ridges,
softening it with showers,
and blessing its growth . . .
The pastures of the wilderness drip,
the hills gird themselves with joy,
the meadows clothe themselves with flocks,
the valleys deck themselves with grain,
they shout and sing together for joy.

PSALMS, 65: 9-13

For keenest enjoyment, I visit the [flowering cherry trees] when the dew is on them, or in cloudy weather, or when the rain is falling; and I must be alone or with someone who cares for them as I do.

DAVID FAIRCHILD

When it rained in the afternoons, children were allowed to eat their mangoes in the garden, stripped naked and dancing about, first getting sticky with mango juice and then getting slippery with rain.

SARA SULERI

Then, wriggling our toes in the mud like eight-year-olds, we closed the garden gate, wiped our feet on the lawn grass, lifted our faces, eyes shut, mouths wide, drank the rain as it fell, and were one with grass and trees.

HAL BORLAND

But next day the sun is early hot. The wet hay streams and is sweet. The beams pour into a southward coombe of the hills and the dense yew is warm as a fruit-wall, so that the utmost of fragrance is extracted from the marjoram and thyme and fanned by the coming and going of the butterflies. . . .

EDWARD THOMAS

Through the slow summer, when the sun
         Called to each frond and whorl
That all he could for flowers was being done,
         Why did it not uncurl?

THOMAS HARDY

Where are the little yellow aconites of eight weeks ago? I neither know nor care. They were sunny and the sun shines, and sunniness means change, and petals passing and coming.

D. H. LAWRENCE

Last night, there came a frost, which has done great damage to my garden. . . . It is sad that Nature will play such tricks with us poor mortals, inviting us with sunny smiles to confide in her, and them, when we are entirely within her power, tricking us to the heart.

NATHANIEL HAWTHORNE

Any night now frost may blacken the last crotalarias, zinnias, marigolds, and chrysanthemums. But, when the dead branches have been cleared away, there will still be the green of the ivy, the grey of santolina, and the scarlet fruit of the firethorn.

ELIZABETH LAWRENCE

NAMING THE PLANTS

. . . The old vernacular names [of flowers] are the connecting links between us and the flower lovers of all the ages—men, women, and children, a long line of them—stretching across the years through countless gardens, high and humble, through woods and meadows and marshes to the little gatherings of potent herbs and edible roots nestled against the protecting walls of ancient monasteries wherein were kept the first records of flowers and their names.

LOUISE BEEBE WILDER

All the names I know from nurse:
Gardener's garters, Shepherd's purse,
Bachelor's buttons, Lady's smock,
And the Lady Hollyhock.

ROBERT LOUIS STEVENSON

Seeing the garden at Rose Cottage Barbie realized she had always longed for one. She was ashamed of her ignorance of the names and natures of plants.

PAUL SCOTT

Over yonder were what she called her "word plants"—the wild flowers she planted because they had names she liked. Creepin' Charlie, Lizzie run by the fence, love's a-bustin', fetch me some ivy cause Baby's got the croup. . . .

OLIVE ANN BURNS

Many fine flowers are cursed with atrocious names. I'd just as soon call an iris "Cystitis" as to call it a name inspired by some gasbag politician or some movie queen who wouldn't know her namesake's pistil from its stamens.

JULIAN R. MEADE

[Scholars] Love not the flower they pluck, and know it not, And all their botany is Latin names.

RALPH WALDO EMERSON

Coming to a clump of dried branches cut close to the ground, she paused to catch her breath, really stumped to remember what had been planted in that place the preceding year. As she closed her eyes in an endeavor to capture the lost mouthful, the little boy came to her rescue. "Never mind, mother," he said, "don't rack your brains, call it Deadium stickium" and that is the way names are born.

LOUISE SEYMOUR JONES

If you are a beginner try not to be worried about the name problem. You will never know all the names. Nobody does. At least if there are such people they don't have time to garden.

GEOFFREY B. CHARLESWORTH

FROM

CONTENT IN A GARDEN

BY
CANDACE WHEELER

IT IS CURIOUS TO NOTE how much of love and appreciation certain flowers owe to certain poets. I have a friend who has made a "Shakespeare garden," in which nothing grows which the great magician has not noticed or praised. One may find there all of poor Ophelia's flowers and herbs,—things with beautiful names like rosemary and thyme and basil; but I am constrained to confess that they make far less show in the garden than is warranted by the impression they have made upon the mind.

There is surely many a daisy border which exists by virtue of the one "modest crimson-tippèd flower" which came to grief under the ploughshare of Robbie Burns. And how much of the love of the succeeding generations do daffodils and primroses owe to the loving verse of Herrick,—to the tender likening of them to "children young, speaking with tears before ye have a tongue." As for roses and lilies and violets, it seems to me a library of poems could be made which name or praise or liken them to human roses or lilies or violets. Indeed, in certain rare collections there is a book filled from cover to cover with tributes in all languages and from all periods to the rose. It is not the least of the tokens of the royalty and dominion of the rose, that the choicest of the sensations which we call color is called by its name. We use it to describe a sunset sky or the tinting of a baby's finger-tips; and even the innumerable variations of shades of dyes of damasks and velvet and precious silken stuffs which commend their tints to human eyes, rose-color describes, and the flower mingles its remembrance with the loveliest of them all.

Rose-color leads the list of color names suggested by flowers in frequency of use; lavender, which comes next and covers as great a range of tints, is named from an herb which few know by sight, and of which, in fact, the most familiar association is a literary one. One knows it chiefly from English poets and writers—from lavender "strewings" and lavendered linen of English song and story. But it is in my garden, its tall, straight stalks grown out of dried and withered seeds which came to me in a letter from a woman whose face I have never seen. Violet and heliotrope are in the same range of tint that we call lavender, but we find their namesakes in every garden. We should have to invent new words for our color sensations, if we could not use the names of flowers and fruits. But, after all, how came their names? How came the word and the thing together ere they began their long travel down through the ages?

We may fancy that Eve—herself the first rose of womanhood—gave its name among the roses of Eden, and we like to think that as Adam "gave names to all cattle," Eve tried her syllables upon the flowers.

But there were many outside flower-sisters, straggling afar from the closed limits of Eden, who awaited their names until the world was peopled, and then found them by virtue of the associations they touched and the sensations they evoked. We can almost trace the state and doings of mankind in their names. The sunflower suggests sun-worship, and the iris smacks of Pagan days, and the fleur-de-lis of banners and royal pageants; marigold and lady's-slipper and jewel-weed came into speech after the vanities were born and well grown among the daughters of men, but the lilies and roses and violets and daffodils of early English verse are inalienably ours, and belong to our race history, even although they might have begun in Eden, or at its very gates. Wake-robin, larkspur, and crowfoot, these smack of rustic observation and nature-love, of love of birds and living things. They have not been named from characteristics, but from form and likeness and faint suggestion. But it is not the same with herbs. Rue and sage, and summer savory! Human emotion and human wisdom, and human satisfaction are behind them all; boneset is physical healing, caraway is mental philosophy, balm is for blessing, and pennyroyal is a lesson on the height possible to loneliness and poverty. And so through all the familiar names which come to us in long tradition, names given by rustic peoples who lived near the sod and whose experiences were of nature.

But among all the names of all flowers, none ever appealed so surely to an experienced soul as heart's-ease. Heart's-ease! There is in it so profound a sense of world-sorrow, so tender an acceptance of comfort! . . . .

The scientific names of flowers are a painful necessity; common names represent their relation to humanity, Latin names only scientific facts. When some clever friend gives me the Latin name of a favorite of my garden, and it immediately drops in and out of my consciousness, I comfort myself by remembering that Charlotte Cushman once said, she could "only remember two Latin words, and those were delirium tremens." Nevertheless I feel a lurking consciousness that it is hardly respectable not to know the Latin names and remote ancestry of things which you live with, just as it argues a certain culpable indifference to one's forebearers—to those of our line who lived and loved and were responsible for our being—not to treasure their brief history and connection, and make a family catechism of their names for our children and our children's children.

A BOUQUET OF BEAUTIES

Forsythia is pure joy. There is not an ounce, not a glimmer of sadness or even *knowledge* in forsythia. Pure, undiluted, untouched joy.

ANNE MORROW LINDBERGH

I do not think I have ever seen anything more beautiful than the bluebell I have been looking at. I know the beauty of our Lord by it.

GERARD MANLEY HOPKINS

In the dooryard fronting an old farm-house near the white-wash'd palings,
Stands the lilac-bush tall-growing with heart-shaped leaves of rich green,
With many a pointed blossom rising delicate, with the perfume strong I love,
With every leaf a miracle. . . .

WALT WHITMAN

We usually think of a Poppy as a coarse flower; but it is the most transparent and delicate of all the blossoms of the field. The rest, nearly all of them, depend upon the texture of their surfaces for color. But the Poppy is painted glass; it never glows so brightly as when the sun shines through it. Wherever it is seen, against the light or with the light, always it is a flame, and warms the wind like a blown ruby.

CELIA THAXTER

And then we have *Alyssum* . . . its little bunches of tiny white flowers smell exactly like new mown hay, particularly when the sun shines hot upon them or after a shower. It is good, as every gardener knows, as an edger or as a carpeter; and how the bees love it!

LOUISE BEEBE WILDER

"Do you know what I found, yesterday, at the end of the garden under the chestnut tree? A little clump of tiny tiny cyclamen. I hadn't the heart to pick them. They are too beautiful.". . . Alix did not admit that she had fallen to her knees by the miracle of the cyclamen, and spoken to them.

MARGARET DRABBLE

Imitating the grownups who were never without a cigarette hanging from their mouths, we would pick the tightly wrapped buds of the hibiscus flowers, which, with their red tips, looked to us like lighted cigarettes.

JUDITH ORTIZ COFER

I smelt the violets in her hand and asked, half in words, half in signs, a question which meant, "Is love the sweetness of flowers?"

HELEN KELLER

... Here's flowers for you;
Hot lavender, mints, savory, marjoram;
The marigold, that goes to bed wi' the sun
And with him rises weeping . . .
. . . daffodils
That come before the swallow dares, and take
The winds of March with beauty; violets dim,
But sweeter than the lids of Juno's eyes
Or Cytherea's breath; pale primroses,
That die unmarried, ere they can behold
Bright Phoebus in his strength, a malady
Most incident to maids; bold oxlips and
The crown imperial; lilies of all kinds,
The flower-de-luce being one!

WILLIAM SHAKESPEARE

The Grape Hyacinth is the favorite spring flower of my
garden—but no! I thought a minute ago the Scilla was! and
what place has the Violet? the Flower de Luce? I cannot
decide, but this I know—it is some blue flower.

ALICE MORSE EARLE

Dazzling white the picotees shone; the golden-eyed marigolds glittered;
the nasturtiums wreathed the veranda poles in green and gold flame. If
only one had time to look at these flowers long enough, time to get over

the sense of novelty and strangeness, time to know them! But as soon as one paused to part the petals, to discover the underside of the leaf, along came Life and one was swept away.

KATHERINE MANSFIELD

We are so used to flowers wrapped up in the pretty envelopes of their corollas and calyces, so softened in our taste for the lovely in Nature, that we scarcely rate an alder catkin as a flower at all. Yet it is nothing else. . . .

DONALD CULROSS PEATTIE

One cannot praise the pond-lily; his best words mar it, like the insects that eat its petals: but he can contemplate it as it opens in the morning sun and distills such perfume, such purity, such snow of petal and such gold of anther, from the dark water and still darker ooze.

JOHN BURROUGHS

The big bright leaves lay calm upon the water, and calmer yet upon the leaves lay the lilies, white and yellow. When they were buds, they were like white and gold birds sleeping, head under wing, or like summat carven out of glistering stone. . . . But when they were come into full blow they wunna like anything but themselves, and they were so lovely you couna choose but cry to see them.

MARY WEBB

I hope that it is still alive, and that it will go on living for a long time, that flourishing, irrepressible despot, a centenarian at least twice over: the wisteria that spills over the garden walls of the house where I was born, and down into the rue des Vignes.

COLETTE

What is the lily and all of the rest
Of the flowers to a man with a heart in his breast,
That was dipped brimmin' full of the honey and dew
Of the sweet clover-blossoms his babyhood knew?

JAMES WHITCOMB RILEY

It is as sprightly as the daffodil, as colorful as the rose, as resolute as the zinnia, as delicate as the chrysanthemum, as aggressive as the petunia, as ubiquitous as the violet, and as stately as the snap-dragon. . . . Since it is native to America, and nowhere else in the world, and common to every state in the Union, I present the American marigold for designation as the national floral emblem of our country.

EVERETT M. DIRKSEN

Look to the blowing Rose about us—"Lo,
Laughing," she says, "into the world I blow,
        At once the silken tassel of my Purse
Tear, and its Treasure on the Garden throw."

EDWARD FITZGERALD

Sweet rose, whose hue, angry and brave,
    Bids the rash gazer wipe his eye:
Thy root is ever in its grave,
        And thou must die.

GEORGE HERBERT

. . . For a rose garden should be in its season a wonder to be
sought, as, when its season is past, it is a wilderness to be
avoided. . . .

JAMES SHIRLEY HIBBERD

God made a little gentian;
It tried to be a rose
And failed, and all the summer laughed.
But just before the snows
There came a purple creature
That ravished all the hill;
And summer hid her forehead,
And mockery was still.

EMILY DICKINSON

ALL THE YEAR 'ROUND

... All seasons shall be sweet to thee,
Whether the summer clothes the general earth
With greenness, or the redbreast sit and sing
Betwixt the tufts of snow on the bare branch
Of mossy apple-tree, while the nigh thatch
Smokes in the sun-thaw. . . .

SAMUEL TAYLOR COLERIDGE

There are snowdrops coming out in the garden, and spring is
on the way. I shall see it. . . . And because I am alive, I shall
watch it all happen and be part of the miracle.

ROSAMUNDE PILCHER

Those of us who are gardeners do not need to train ourselves to be
aware of the seasons, intuitively or any other way, for the seasons have
us by the throat.

GERMAINE GREER

There is the almond blossom in February, and a few weeks of
pre-spring panic in the garden as we try to do the word we've
been talking about all winter.

PETER MAYLE

Say, on the noon when the half-sunny hours told that April was nigh,
And I upgathered and cast forth the snow from the crocus-border,
Fashioned and furbished the soil into a summer-seeming order,
Glowing in gladsome faith that I quickened the year thereby.

THOMAS HARDY

Yukiko circled the flower bed, inspected the budding
branches of the lilac by the pond, picked up the cat Bell, and
knelt for a moment under a round-clipped gardenia bush. . . .
She would soon be called back to Tokyo, and . . . she hated
to leave spring in this garden behind. And she was perhaps
praying that she might still be here to see the lilac in blossom.

JUNICHIRO TANIZAKI

If spring came but once in a century, instead of once a year, or burst
forth with the sound of an earthquake, and not in silence, what wonder
and expectation there would be in all hearts to behold the miraculous
change! But now the silent succession suggests nothing but necessity.
To most men only the cessation of the miracle would be miraculous,
and the perpetual exercise of God's power seems less wonderful
than its withdrawal would be.

HENRY WADSWORTH LONGFELLOW

She went up to the chestnut tree and leaned her head against its trunk. Perhaps she could hear the sap rising and the flowers preparing to burst out of the buds. *Not one of all those ravenous hours, but thee devours?* Well, yes, that was true still, but it mattered less on a spring morning.

BARBARA PYM

For lo, the winter is past, the rain is over and gone;
The flowers appear on the earth, the time of singing has come
and the voice of the turtledove is heard in our land.
The fig tree puts forth its figs, and the vines are in blossom;
they give forth fragrance.
Arise my love, my fair one,
and come away.

THE SONG OF SOLOMON, 2:11-13

So then the year is repeating its old story again. We are come once more, thank God! to its most charming chapter. The violets and the May flowers are as its inscriptions or vignettes. It always makes a pleasant impression on us, when we open again at these pages of the book of life.

JOHANN WOLFGANG VON GOETHE

Spring unlocks the flowers to paint the laughing soil.

REGINALD HEBER

Sweet spring, full of sweet days and roses, a box where sweets compacted lie.

GEORGE HERBERT

Every year, back Spring comes, with the nasty little birds yapping their fool heads off, and the ground all mucked up with arbutus. Year after year after year.

DOROTHY PARKER

Spring makes it own statement, so loud and clear that the gardener seems to be only one of the instruments, not the composer.

GEOFFREY B. CHARLESWORTH

I always think that this, the time of Tulips, is the season of all the year when the actual arranging of flowers affords the greatest pleasure. The rush and heat of summer have not yet come; the days are still fairly restful, and one is so glad to greet and handle these early blossoms.

GERTRUDE JEKYLL

May and June. Soft syllables, gentle names for the two best months in the garden year: cool, misty mornings gently burned away with a warming spring sun, followed by breezy afternoons and chilly nights. The discussion of philosophy is over, it's time for work to begin. . . .

PETER LOEWER

In June as many as a dozen species may burst their buds on a single day. No man can heed all of these anniversaries; no man can ignore all of them.

ALDO LEOPOLD

June is, above all things, "leafy," seeming chiefly to concentrate her energies on her foliage; for although she really is not lacking in flowers, they are almost swamped in the great green flood which has swept silently but irresistibly across the land.

FRANCES T. DANA

There are some moments when I feel pleased with my garden, and other moments when I despair. The pleased moments usually happen in spring, and last up to the middle of June. By that time all the freshness has gone off; everything has become heavy; everything has lost that adolescent look, that look of astonishment at its own youth. The middle-aged spread has begun.

VITA SACKVILLE-WEST

Spring flowers are long since gone. Summer's bloom hangs limp on every terrace. The gardener's feet drag a bit on the dusty path and the hinge in his back is full of creaks.

LOUISE SEYMOUR JONES

On this day, summer, languishing but not really sick, receives her visitors with a certain deliberateness—a pretty girl who knows she doesn't need to stay in bed. The yellow squash illuminates the aging vine, the black-billed cuckoo taps out his hollow message in code (a series of three dots), and zinnias stand as firm and quiet as old valorous deeds.

E. B. WHITE

Through the thick corn the scarlet poppies peep,
And round green roots and yellowing stalks I see
     Pale blue convolvulus in tendrils creep:
        And air-swept lindens yield
Their scent, and rustle down their perfumed showers
     Of bloom on the bent grass where I am laid,
     And bower me from the August sun with shade. . . .

MATTHEW ARNOLD

For man, autumn is a time of harvest, of gathering together.
For nature, it is a time of sowing, of scattering abroad.

EDWIN WAY TEALE

Season of mists and mellow fruitfulness,
     Close bosom-friend of the maturing sun;
Conspiring with him how to load and bless
     With fruit the vines that round the thatch-eaves run;
To bend with apples the mossed cottage-trees,
     And fill all fruit with ripeness to the core. . . .

JOHN KEATS

For gardeners, this is the season of lists and callow
hopefulness; hundreds of thousands of bewitched readers
are poring over their catalogues, making lists of their
seed and plant orders, and dreaming their dreams.

KATHERINE S. WHITE

Normal people admire sugar maples or watch football games in fall. My taste runs more toward combating seasonal senescence in the garden, delaying the inevitable, and more positively, preserving beauty. Summer in the North is too short, and I don't see any reason to throw in the trowel on Labor Day. . . .

FREDERICK MCGOURTY

But now in September the garden has cooled, and with it my possessiveness. The sun warms my back instead of beating on my head. . . . The harvest has dwindled, and I have grown apart from the intense midsummer relationship that brought it on.

ROBERT FINCH

I love the fall. I love it because of the smells that you speak of; and also because things are dying, things that you don't have to take care of any more, and the grass stops growing.

MARK VAN DOREN

. . . When September lines the road-sides of New England with the purple of the aster, and flings its mantle of golden-rod over her hills, and fills her hollows with the pink drifts of the Joe-Pye-weed or with the intense red-purple of the iron-weed, and guards her brooks with tall ranks of yellow sunflowers, then I think that any moor or meadow of Great Britain might be set in her midst and yet fail to pale her glory.

FRANCES T. DANA

The grim frost is at hand, when the apples will fall
thick, almost thundrous, on the hardened earth.

D. H. LAWRENCE

In the sheltered heart of the clumps last year's foliage still
clings to the lower branches, tatters of orange that mutter with
the passage of the wind, the talk of old women warning the
green generation of what they, too, must come to when
the sap runs back.

JACQUETTA HAWKES

From December to March, there are for many of us three gardens—the
garden outdoors, the garden of pots and bowls in the house, and the
garden of the mind's eye. . . .

KATHERINE S. WHITE

There are two seasonal diversions that can ease the bite of any
winter. One is the January thaw. The other is the seed catalogues.

HAL BORLAND

THE ART OF NATURE

By means of microscopic observation and astronomical projection the lotus flower can become the foundation for an entire theory of the universe and an agent whereby we may perceive Truth.

YUKIO MISHIMA

We seem to make it our study to recede from Nature, not only in the various tonsure of greens into the most regular and formal shapes, but even in monstrous attempts beyond the reach of the art itself: we run into sculpture, and are yet better pleased to have our Trees in the most awkward figures of men and animals, than in the most regular of their own.

ALEXANDER POPE

Nothing is more completely the child of art than a garden.

SIR WALTER SCOTT

What a bewitching land [France] is! What a garden! Surely the leagues of bright green lawns are swept and brushed and watered every day and their grasses trimmed by the barber. Surely the hedges are shaped and measured and their symmetry preserved by the most architectural of gardeners.

MARK TWAIN

"We are to walk about your gardens, and gather the strawberries ourselves, and sit under trees;—and whatever else you may like to provide, it is to be all out of doors—a table spread in the shade, you know. Every thing as natural and simple as possible. Is not that your idea?"

"Not quite. My idea of the simple and the natural will be to have the table spread in the dining-room. The nature and the simplicity of gentlemen and ladies, with their servants and furniture, I think is best observed by meals within doors. When you are tired of eating strawberries in the garden, there shall be cold meat in the house."

JANE AUSTEN

Let us a little permit Nature to take her own way; she better understands her own affairs than we.

MICHEL EYQUEM DE MONTAIGNE

At Christmas I no more desire a rose
Than wish a snow in May's newfangled mirth;
But like of each thing that in season grows.

WILLIAM SHAKESPEARE

These roses under my window make no reference to former roses or to better ones; they are for what they are; they exist with God to-day. There is no time to them. There is simply the rose; it is perfect in every moment of its existence.

RALPH WALDO EMERSON

'Tis all enforced, the fountain and the grot,
    While the sweet fields do lie forgot,
Where willing Nature does to all dispense
    A wild and fragrant innocence.

ANDREW MARVELL

Gardening is always more or less a warfare against nature.
It is true we go over to the "other side" for a few hints, but we
might as well abandon our spades and pitchforks as pretend
that nature is everything and art nothing.

JAMES SHIRLEY HIBBERD

. . . The imaginations excited by the view of an unknown and untravelled
wilderness are not such as arise in the artificial solitude of parks and
gardens, a flattering notion of self-sufficiency, a placid indulgence
of voluntary delusions, a secure expansion of the fancy, or a cool
concentration of the mental powers. The phantoms which haunt
a desert are want, and misery, and danger. . . .

SAMUEL JOHNSON

Just when the daffodils have quit and the azaleas are blooming
like crazy in the front yards of half the split-levels within 350
miles, the field offers a sight that to my mind is worth most of
the azaleas in town (and all its hydrangeas)—a strip of land
some fifty feet wide, where the owner has held back the tractor
that annually mows the rest of his property.

ALLEN LACY

There were only wildflowers on this property, and a great press of wild and unruly trees, brush that had begun creeping close to the buildings and thickets barely held back by stone walls. The sense of sheer green abundance was overpowering. Nature may once have allowed this small human clearing in its midst, but it had obviously begun to reconsider.
DIANE ACKERMAN

My idea of gardening is to discover something wild in my wood and weed around it with the utmost care until it has a chance to grow and spread.
MARGARET BOURKE-WHITE

Living Nature, not dull Art
Shall plan my ways and rule my Heart.
JOHN HENRY CARDINAL NEWMAN

WHY WE GARDEN

Life begins the day you start a garden.
CHINESE PROVERB

To dwell is to garden.
MARTIN HEIDEGGER

A garden really lives only insofar as it is an expression of faith, the embodiment of a hope and a song of praise.

RUSSELL PAGE

I am led to reflect how much more delightful to an undebauched mind, is the task of making improvements on the earth, than all the vain glory which can be acquired from ravaging it, by the most uninterrupted career of conquests.

GEORGE WASHINGTON

We learn from our gardens to deal with the most urgent question of the time: How much is enough?

WENDELL BERRY

In the ancient world it was ever the greatest of the emperors and the wisest of the philosophers that sought peace and rest in a garden.

SIR GEORGE SITWELL

"I have no more than twenty acres of ground," he replied, "the whole of which I cultivate myself with the help of my children; and our labor keeps off from us three great evils, boredom, vice, and want."

VOLTAIRE

A love of flowers would beget early rising, industry, habits of close observation, and of reading. It would incline the mind to notice natural phenomena, and to reason upon them. It would occupy the mind with pure thoughts, and inspire a sweet and gentle enthusiasm; maintain simplicity of taste; and . . . unfold in the heart an enlarged, unstraitened, ardent piety.

HENRY WARD BEECHER

I flatter myself the Ladies would soon think that their vacant Hours in the Culture of the *Flower-Garden* would be more innocently spent and with greater Satisfaction than the common Talk over a Tea-Table where Envy and Detraction so commonly preside. Whereas when Opportunity and Weather invite them amongst their Flowers, there they may dress, and admire and cultivate Beauties like themselves without *envying* or *being envied.*

JOHN LAWRENCE

I think more and more people are taking to gardening to get away from the horrors of life. At least in the garden there is peace. All I need is no interruptions. What I really welcome is a postal strike.

FREDERICK ASHTON

A garden is the best alternative therapy.

GERMAINE GREER

. . . Just for one's health . . . it is very necessary to work in the garden and to see the flowers growing.

VINCENT VAN GOGH

Surely Nature, as it is understood in the usual slapdash way, as human, if not dilettante, *experience* (hiking in a national park, jogging on the beach at dawn, even tending, with the usual comical frustrations, a suburban garden), is wonderfully consoling; a place where, when you go there, it has to take you in?

JOYCE CAROL OATES

What was particularly nice about the garden was that, at any moment, standing in the narrow paths or amidst the bushes and trees, Chance could start to wander, never knowing whether he was going forward or backward, unsure whether he was ahead of or behind his previous steps. All that mattered was moving in his own time, like the growing plants.

JERZY KOSINSKI

Let no one think that real gardening is a bucolic and meditative occupation. It is an insatiable passion, like everything else to which a man gives his heart.

KAREL CAPEK

... No man but feels more of a man in the world if he have a bit of ground that he can call his own. However small it is on the surface, it is four thousand miles deep; and that is a very handsome property.

CHARLES DUDLEY WARNER

Farm children have little love for Nature and are surprisingly ignorant about wildflowers, save a very few varieties. The child who is garden bred has a happier start in life, a greater love and knowledge of Nature.

ALICE MORSE EARLE

When all is said and done, is there any more wonderful sight, any moment when man's reason is nearer to some sort of contact with the nature of the world than the sowing of seeds, the planting of cuttings, the transplanting of shrubs or the grafting of slips?

ST. AUGUSTINE

Lord make us mindful of the little things that grow and blossom in these days to make the world beautiful for us.

W. E. DUBOIS

... The public must learn how to cherish the nobler and rarer plants, and to plant the aloe, able to wait a hundred years for its bloom, or its garden will contain, presently, nothing but potatoes and pot-herbs.

MARGARET FULLER

When, as a very small child, I was playing with a horsetail that had been growing as a weed in one of our flower-beds, dismantling it section by section like a constructional toy, I remember how my father told me it was one of the oldest plants on earth, and I experienced a curious confusion of time. I was holding the oldest plant in my hand, and so I, too, was old.

JACQUETTA HAWKES

To cultivate a garden is to walk with God.

CHRISTIAN NESTELL BOVEE

The kiss of the sun for pardon,
The song of the birds for mirth,
One is nearer God's Heart in a garden
Than anywhere else on earth.

DOROTHY FRANCES GURNEY

Flower in the crannied wall,
I pluck you out of the crannies;—
I hold you here, root and all, in my hand,
Little flower—but if I could understand
What you are, root and all, and all in all,
I should know what God and man is.

ALFRED TENNYSON

Gardening is the only unquestionably useful job.

GEORGE BERNARD SHAW

There is a class of men who would pare everything to the mere grade of *utility,* who think it the height of wisdom to ask, when one manifests an enthusiasm in the culture of flowers, "of what use are they?" With such we have no sympathy.

JOSEPH BRECK

Sweet-pea seeds contain a poison that can keep a person bedridden for months. The night-blooming jimson has enough power in its leave to produce delirium. Daffodil bulbs when eaten cause stomach cramps. . . . But the conclusion drawn by the writer of the article, chewing absently on a daffodil bulb, was a good one. *We must plant this garden anyway.* Even in the face of such terrors, we must plant this garden.

E. B. WHITE

He places a seed in the dust for the reason
That it may in the day of distress, give fruit.

SADI

Who sows a field, or trains a flower,
Or plants a tree, is more than all.

JOHN GREENLEAF WHITTIER

Gardening takes a plot of land, a hoe and willing muscles. Scratching the soil, harvesting garden fruits, are peaceful pursuits. With a garden, there is hope.

GRACE FIRTH

Shall I not have intelligence with the earth? Am I not partly leaves and vegetable mould myself?

HENRY DAVID THOREAU

I am a part of all you see
In Nature: part of all you feel:
I am the impact of the bee
Upon the blossom; in the tree
I am the sap—that shall reveal
The leaf, the bloom—that flows and flutes
Up from the darkness through its roots.

MADISON CAWEIN

I no longer say, as I once did, "I have to work in the garden today." I say, with deep contentment, "I'm gardening today." I have truly reaped the bounty of the garden.

MARTHA STEWART

Sometimes since I've been in the garden I've looked up through the trees at the sky and I have had a strange feeling of being happy as if something were pushing and drawing and making me breathe fast. Magic is always pushing and drawing and making things out of nothing. Everything is made out of Magic, leaves and trees, flowers and birds, badgers and foxes and squirrels and people. So it must be all round us. In this garden—in all the places.

FRANCES HODGSON BURNETT

INDEX

Gardens

More, Sir Thomas (1478–1535), English statesman and author, 14

Morris, William (1834–1896), English artist and poet, 50

Morrison, Toni (b. 1931), American writer, 83

Munro, Eleanor (b. 1928), American art historian, 21, 43, 52

Murdoch, Iris (b. 1919), Irish-born writer, 37

Narayan, R.K. (b. 1906), Indian writer, 23

Neugeboren, Jay (b. 1938), American writer, 36

Newman, John Henry (1801–1890), English theologian and writer, 13, 139

Nursery rhyme, Anonymous, 57

O'Keeffe, Georgia (1887–1986), American painter, 37

Oates, Joyce Carol (b. 1938), American writer, 142

Orwell, George (1903–1950), English writer, 15

Osler, Mirabel (20th-century) English garden writer, 37, 82, 110

Ostenso, Martha (1900–1963), 70

Page, Ruth (20th-century) garden expert, 18

Page, Russell (1906–1985), American landscape architect the education of a gardener, 140

Parker, Dorothy (1893–1967), American humorist, 131

Parker, Theodore (1810–1860), American Unitarian theologian, 60, 67

Peattie, Donald Culross (1898–1964), American botanist and writer, 125

Percy, Walker (1916–1990), American writer and philosopher, 23, 90

Perényi, Eleanor (b. 1918), American writer, 19, 69, 103

Perrin, Noel (b. 1927), American writer, 68

Pettingill, Amos (William Harris, 1900–1981), American nurseryman, 35, 56, 109

Pilcher, Rosamunde (b. 1924), English writer, 128

Pliny the Elder (23–79 A.D.), Roman naturalist, 44, 58

Pope, Alexander (1688–1744), English poet, 136

Price, Nancy (20th-century) American writer, 98

Proust, Marcel (1871–1922), French writer, 41

Proverb, Chinese, 19, 139

Proverb, Welsh, 80

Proverbs 24:30–31, 32

Pyle, Robert Michael (b. 1947), American writer, 101

Pym, Barbara (1913–1980), English writer, 130

Quindlen, Anna (b. 1953), American writer, 19

Rau, Santha Rama (b. 1923), Indian-born writer, 42

Rawlings, Marjorie Kinnan (1896–1953), American writer, 59, 104

ONE HUNDRED FIFTY FOUR

Perennial pleasures plants,
wholesome harvest reaps.

Bronson Alcott

I would love to be transported
scented Elizabethan garden
herbs and Honeysuckles, a
garden and Roses clambering
over a simple arbour....

Rosemary Verey

For the garden is not only a p
which to make things grow
display the beautiful flowers
th, but a place in which to lau
besides, should have a hidden
in which to weep

Alice Lounsber